Not just a GOOD FOOD GUIDE
NEW DELHI

M.R. Narayan Swamy

D0910923

Marshall Cavendish
Editions

PHOTO CREDITS

Marshall Cavendish International (Asia) Pte Ltd: pages 28, 34, 96, 123 (from *Vegetarian Feasts*); page 111 (from *Simply Sedap! Chef Wan's Favourite Recipes*); page 152 (from *Chef Wan Around the World*)
All other photos by Keshav Chaturvedi

Editor: Lee Mei Lin
Designer: Jailani Basari
Cover design: Lynn Chin

**© 2005 Marshall Cavendish International
(Asia) Private Limited**
Published by Marshall Cavendish Editions
An imprint of Marshall Cavendish International (Asia) Private Limited
A member of Times Publishing Limited
Times Centre, 1 New Industrial Road, Singapore 536196
Tel: (65) 6213 9300   Fax: (65) 6285 4871
E-mail: te@sg.marshallcavendish.com
Online Bookstore: www.marshallcavendish.com/genref

**National Library Board (Singapore)
Cataloguing in Publication Data**
Narayan Swamy, M. R.
New Delhi / M. R. Narayan Swamy.
– Singapore : Marshall Cavendish Editions, 2005.
p. cm. – (Not just a good food guide)
Includes indexes.
ISBN : 981-232-996-X
1. Restaurants – India – New Delhi – Guidebooks. 2. New Delhi (India)
– Guidebooks. I. Title. II. Series: Not just a good food guide
TX907.5
647.955456 – dc21   SLS2005020932

Printed in Singapore by Fabulous Printers Pte Ltd

About the Series

For many travellers unacquainted with the intricacies of Asian food, trying the local cuisine in a foreign land is often a daunting task. Add to that the language barrier and many tourists return home with the notion that there is little variety in Asian food or that hotel food is the epitome of what is available.

The series was conceived to help travellers unfamiliar with the local language and cuisine overcome this obstacle. Each book starts out with an overview of the eating habits and customs in that particular city or country. The food of each destination is then presented in a fashion that Westerners can relate to — by food group such as appetisers, salads, rice, noodles, meats and desserts. In some cases, food is categorised by cooking style such as stewed or grilled food. In addition, a short write-up is provided for each local dish, explaining what the most authentic version usually contains.

In many Asian cities, the most authentic and best versions of a dish are often found in some dark, dingy corner of the city that even the locals will find difficult to locate. For safety reasons, the books in the series will focus on outlets that are easily accessible and will not cause visitors to be stranded and fearing for their lives. While most of the outlets recommended by our authors are in the mid-price range, a few on the higher end of the scale have been included to give readers a wider option.

As the world grows smaller, it is inevitable that the foods of other countries, Asian or Western, find a place in the local culinary scene. For this reason, each book will have a section on international foods and where they can be found.

It is our hope that this series will help to open a new world of tastes to all travellers.

Contents

HOW TO USE THIS GUIDE

Restaurant listings

The restaurants in this book have been grouped according to the type of cuisine they offer: north Indian, south Indian, Chinese and International. The listings for them can be found at the end of each main section. Within each listing, restaurants appear in alphabetical order. All restaurants are recommended by the author except for those under the International listings, which were recommended by his friends. The author's top picks are indicated with a special icon.

The icons used in this book:

Author's choice picks.

Address.

Approximate distance from Imperial Hotel, Janpath, in Connaught Place, which lies in the very heart of Delhi. Where 'walking distance' is indicated, this would mean a distance of about half a kilometre or less.

Operating hours. Delhi restaurants and eateries open till late into the night. Last orders can be placed 30 minutes before closing time.

Telephone number. To call a restaurant from a land line within Delhi, all you need to do is dial the number directly. If you are outside the city or using a mobile telephone, add 011 (city code) to the number.

Home delivery service. Several restaurants offer this service for a minimum order and within a select area. Call the restaurant directly for orders.

Restaurants that serve purely vegetarian meals. Such places do not serve alcohol or meat. There are no vegan options in the city.

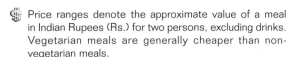

💲 Price ranges denote the approximate value of a meal in Indian Rupees (Rs.) for two persons, excluding drinks. Vegetarian meals are generally cheaper than non-vegetarian meals.

💲 below Rs.200

💲 💲 Rs.200 to Rs.400

💲 💲 💲 Rs.400 to Rs.700

💲 💲 💲 💲 Rs.700 to Rs.1000

💲 💲 💲 💲 💲 Rs.1000 to Rs.1500

💲 💲 💲 💲 💲 💲 above Rs.1500

Mode of payment. Not all restaurants in the city accept credit cards and those that do may not accept all cards. Please call in advance to check.

ab Almost all restaurants, even the smallest, carry menus written in English.

HALAL FOOD

One of the legacies left behind by the Mughal emperors is the firm entrenchment of Islam in India. There are thus many Muslim-owned restaurants in Delhi and these serve *halal* food, or food that is permissible. Food that is not permissible, or *haram*, include alcohol and pork (including its by-products). Where non-Muslim Indian food outlets offering non-vegetarian cuisine is concerned, note that most use *halal* meat for the simple reason that the majority of butchers in the city are Muslims. There is no independent authority that regulates the provision of *halal* food. If in doubt, please call the restaurant to inquire. The best-known Muslim restaurant listed in this guide is Karim (see pages 86 and 164–166 for more information).

Dial-A-Meal

Dial-A-Meal is a unique company that accepts telephone orders on behalf of select restaurants in Delhi. This is different from home delivery services where you make an order directly with the individual restaurant. The Dial-A-Meal service is applicable only for orders above Rs.300 and there may be restrictions as to the areas they will deliver the food. Call 2984 4444, 2004 2666 or 98181 26444 for enquiries. Several of the recommended restaurants in the listings offer this service.

Finding your way in Delhi

Delhi's public transport system, sad to say, is not top-notch. The city's public buses are always crowded. Although travelling by bus is cheap, visitors would do well to avoid them. The city's buses are partly run by the state and partly by private operators — even then, they are poorly maintained.

Delhi now has a gleaming rail system, but this presently covers a small part of the city that tourists rarely visit. By 2010, however, the rail network should cover most of New Delhi. Until then, the best way to get around is to take a taxi or a three-wheeled auto-rickshaw popularly known as 'auto'.

The good thing about most Delhi vehicles is that they run on compressed natural gas (CNG) and are environmentally friendly, which is ideal because taxis are not air-conditioned while autos leave you open to the elements.

On average, a 10-kilometre ride on an auto should cost about Rs.50 (slightly over US$1) and three times that amount by taxi. There is a radio-operated taxi service, but it is not very popular.

Delhi's taxi and auto drivers are quite a rough lot. Although it is mandatory to operate the fare meter, many choose not to do so especially when the passenger is a foreigner. Hail another taxi. Better still, get the hotel staff to hire a taxi for you. If that is not possible, make sure you discuss and agree on the fare before you get on board.

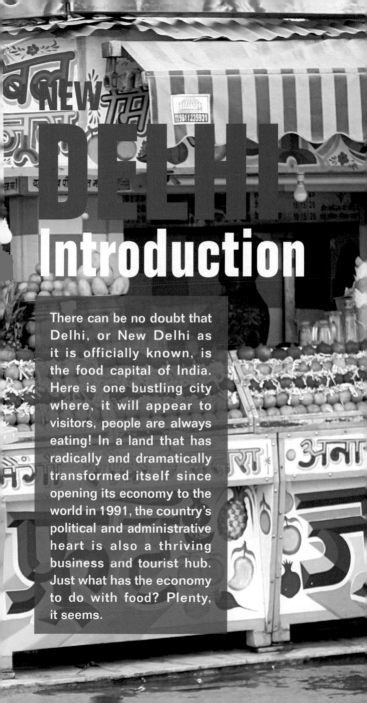

NEW DELHI
Introduction

There can be no doubt that Delhi, or New Delhi as it is officially known, is the food capital of India. Here is one bustling city where, it will appear to visitors, people are always eating! In a land that has radically and dramatically transformed itself since opening its economy to the world in 1991, the country's political and administrative heart is also a thriving business and tourist hub. Just what has the economy to do with food? Plenty, it seems.

For a country where semi-socialist norms were the mainstay for well over four decades, rapid economic liberalisation has led to a boom in business. All this has meant more hotels, more restaurants and more eateries.

There are not only more eateries and restaurants but plenty of variety in the food they offer, too. With more and more Indians travelling to other countries for business or pleasure, there has been a rapid growth in the demand for Italian, Mexican and Middle Eastern cuisine. But then, eating out has always been a way of life in Delhi, a city home to over 15 million people and thousands of food outlets to suit every single pocket. There are so many restaurants, coffee shops and wayside eateries that it is impossible to count them all.

Delhi is a historic city where the infusion of Mughal rule centuries ago brought in its wake a delicious spread of Mughlai food, such as tandoori chicken and mutton biryani, for which the city is so well known. When the 17th-century emperor Shah Jahan constructed the Red Fort in Delhi, a bustling shopping bazaar called Chandni Chowk sprouted in its vicinity. Both the Red Fort and Chandni Chowk still exist. This is the area — crisscrossed by narrow lanes and narrower by-lanes — where Delhi's ever-hungry denizens still go to when they want to satisfy their craving for time-tested dishes whose culinary secrets have been handed down the generations. Not far from Chandni Chowk and near Jama Masjid, India's largest mosque, is a restaurant called Karim. Founded by a man who once served in the kitchen of the last Mughal emperor, Karim is an institution in Delhi's food history. People who profess to love Mughlai cuisine would probably have dined at Karim at least once.

Although Karim is the best-known eatery in Old Delhi (so called because the Mughal-built part of the city preceded the British-designed New Delhi), it is not the only reason to go there. All around Karim are small eateries serving scrumptious fare from sunrise to late at night. Their huge cauldrons and ovens emit an intoxicating aroma of mutton and chicken marinated in the finest of spices.

Delhi's increasing reputation as a haven for food lovers, however, is not just because of Karim or Chandni Chowk. These days every neighbourhood, even residential ones, has at least one restaurant (including the fast food variety!) and several coffee shops offering local and international fare. This bustling city is indeed a food paradise — even pizzas and Tibetan momos can be easily obtained! Most international

food chains are represented here, but they get a run for their money from their Indian counterparts. Even Chinese cuisine, which took off in popularity in the 1980s, is the second most popular after north Indian cuisine. Chinese cuisine has been 'Indianised' to some extent and lovers of Chinese food may be amused by the names that have been given to some Chinese dishes. But this is Delhi where enterprising food merchants have learnt to adapt everything that comes their way — from the time of the Mughals till today — and, in the process, make a tidy profit, too!

Welcome to Delhi!

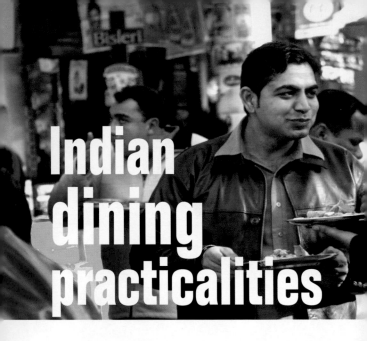

Indian dining practicalities

Part of the fun of foreign travel is experiencing different customs and doing what the locals do in various social settings. It always helps to be prepared though, so here are a few pointers on what to expect when eating out in Delhi.

Using your hands

When it comes to food, do as the Indians do: use your hands to eat. But remember to wash them first. Every eatery would have facilities, however humble, for you to do so. Most restaurants will offer a finger bowl for cleaning your fingers as well as plenty of napkins. Only in the case of small eateries would you need to look for a tap to wash your hands.

When eating, use only your right hand to bring food to your mouth. It is perfectly acceptable to use your left hand to pass food around and serve food, whether for others or for yourself.

For meals where breads like roti, naan or paratha are served, north Indians use their hands to break up the bread and then use the bread to scoop up vegetables and meat. This is done even in expensive restaurants.

For rice meals, however, spoons are used; using the hand to scoop up rice is essentially a south Indian custom.

All restaurants in Delhi, even roadside eateries, will offer spoons and all Chinese eateries will offer forks. Chopsticks are available in Chinese restaurants.

Having a cuppa

If you are dining in a south Indian eatery and have ordered a hot cup of coffee or tea, your drink will come in a stainless steel tumbler sitting inside a *davara,* a squat steel container. If you feel the drink is too hot and you want to cool it down, you can transfer the contents from the cup to the *davara* and back again. Repeat this process several times and your drink will cool very quickly. Where teaspoons are not provided, this transfer process also helps dissolve any sugar you might have added. Many people today choose not to use the *davara.* In a north Indian eatery, your drink will arrive in a mug or china cup and saucer.

For a different atmosphere, head for Barista or Café Coffee Day. These air-conditioned chains are aplenty in the city. They offer several varieties of coffee and tea as well as cakes and pastries. Each outlet also offers amenities of a different sort — chess and Scrabble sets to help you unwind.

Avoiding 'Delhi Belly'

You will get thirsty easily in Delhi's scorching summer months. Be very careful with the water you consume. Many tourists, (even Indians) who complain of upset stomachs — popularly referred to as 'Delhi Belly' — have blamed their illness on the quality of the water. Avoid buying cold drinks from street stalls and small eateries. Take bottled mineral water instead. Even then, buy only reputed brands such as Hello, Kinley or Bisleri. Evian, of course, is available but at a price. If you want an ice-cold fizzy drink, get one that is canned and forgo any extra ice that may be offered.

Paying the bill

- You can ask for the bill when you have finished your meal. In small restaurants where meals cost below Rs.200, it is common to bring the bill up to the cashier and pay there. In bigger restaurants you give the waiter the money or credit card and wait for him to come back to you.

- A sales tax of 12.5 per cent is included in all food bills.

- Credit cards are NOT universally accepted, so be sure to check beforehand if you want to charge it.

Tipping

In a good restaurant, one is expected to tip 10 per cent of the bill. You can leave the tip money on the table, unless you want to tip a particular waiter. At wayside eateries, it is sufficient to top up the bill by Rs.5 to Rs.10.

Other matters

- Orthodox vegetarian restaurants do not serve alcohol.

- When you enter a Chinese restaurant in Delhi, do so with an open mind. The Chinese food you order may not be what you are used to, even though the restaurant says that what is offered is authentic Chinese. Most of the city's Chinese restaurants are run by Indians.

- English is widely spoken in India and so, communicating your needs at restaurants will not be a problem. In fact, it would be best to speak in English rather than attempt to converse in Hindi. Still, here is a list of some expressions which might come in useful. Note that some English words are so common that they have crept into colloquial Hindi.

Useful Hindi expressions

Are you open?	Aap khu lay hain? (AAP khu-LAY hayn?)
Do you take credit cards?	Aap credit cards accept karthe hain? (AAP credit cards accept kar-THE hayn?)
Please bring the menu.	Kripya menu layihe. (Krip-ya menu LA-yee-hay.)
Please bring a bottle of water.	Kripya ek bottle pani layihe. (Krip-ya ek bottle PAA-NEE LA-yee-hay.)
Do you have vegetarian food?	Aapke paas vegetarian khana hain? (AAP-ke paas vegetarian KAH-na hayn?)
Can you make it less hot, please?	Kripya mirchi kum daliye. (Krip-ya mir-chi come DA-lee-yay.)
Can I have the thali, please?	Kripya thali layihe? (Krip-ya THA-lee LA-yee-hay?)
Can I have an empty plate, please?	Kripya ek khali plate dijiye. (Krip-ya ache kha-lee plate DEE-jee-yay.)
Can I have a cup of coffee?	Kripya coffee lahiye. (Krip-ya coffee LA-hee-yay.)
Can we get a child's high chair?	Bachche ke liye kursi mil sukta hai? (Buck-chay ke lee-yay kur-see mil suk-TA hay?
Could we please have the bill?	Kripya bill lahiye. (Krip-ya bill LA-hee-yay.)
Please give me a receipt.	Kripya receipt dijiye. (Krip-ya receipt DEE-jee-yay.)
How much?	Kithna? (KITH-na?)
Where's the toilet?	Toilet kahan hain? (Toilet ka-HAN hayn?)
Where's the sink to wash hands?	Kahan haath clean kar sakte hain? (Ka-han HAATH clean kar suck-te hayn?)
Thank you.	Dhanyavaad. (DHAN-ya-vaad.)
Hello/Goodbye	Namaste (Na-maas-tay)

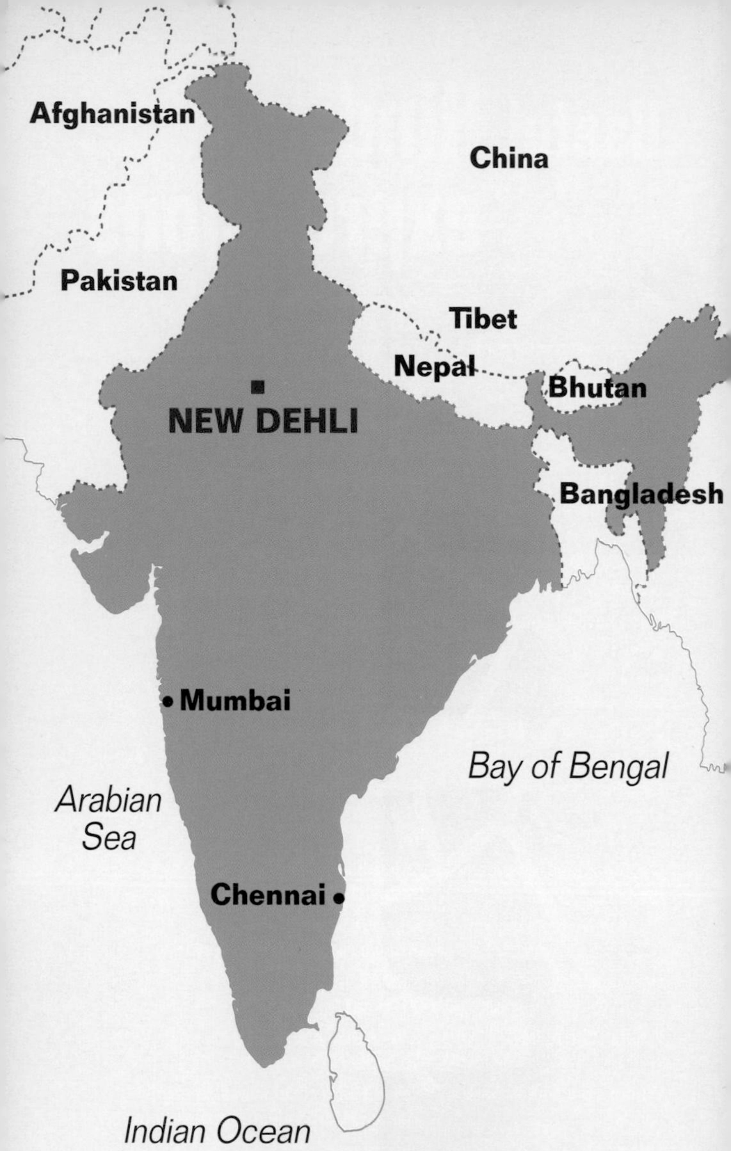

Afghanistan

China

Pakistan

Tibet

Nepal

Bhutan

NEW DEHLI

Bangladesh

Mumbai

Bay of Bengal

Arabian
Sea

Chennai

Indian Ocean

INDIA

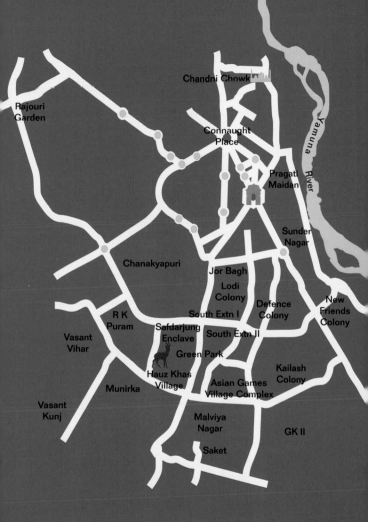

Rajouri
Garden

Chandni Chowk

Connaught
Place

Pragati
Maidan

Yamuna River

Sunder
Nagar

Chanakyapuri

Jor Bagh

Lodi
Colony

Defence
Colony

New
Friends
Colony

South Extn I

R K
Puram

Safdarjung
Enclave

South Extn II

Vasant
Vihar

Green Park

Hauz Khas
Village

Kailash
Colony

Munirka

Asian Games
Village Complex

Vasant
Kunj

Malviya
Nagar

GK II

Saket

NEW DELHI

achaar	pickles
adai	pancake made from dal paste
ajwain	spice; close relative of dill, caraway and cumin
aloo	potato
aloo gobi	dish comprising diced potato and cauliflower
aloo paratha	unleavened wheat bread filled with potatoes
aloo tikki	deep-fried potato and lentil cakes
arhar dal	yellow lentils
asafoetida	pungent spice that comes from dried sap of giant fennel plants
atta	wheat flour
avial	thick south Indian gravy dish consisting of mixed vegetables and grated coconut
badam	almond
basmati	long grained rice used for making **biryani** dishes
besan	flour ground from chickpeas (**chana dal**); also known as chickpea flour and Bengal gram flour; imparts a distinctive flavour; used as a binding agent in Indian cookery
bhath	rice; more commonly known in the north as chaval
bhatura	deep-fried north Indian plain flour bread
bhelpuri	north Indian snack made from deep-fried chickpea flour noodles and flaked rice
biryani	heavy and spicy rice dish cooked together with meat, usually chicken or mutton
bonda	deep-fried potato balls
boondi	tiny fried balls made of gram flour; taken as a snack
chaat	generic term for certain types of snacks such as **golgappa**, **papdi** and **bhelpuri**
chai	tea
chai wala	person who sells tea on the streets

GLOSSARY
of foreign terms

chana dal	chickpeas; also known as Bengal gram and yellow split peas
chana masala	chickpea dish in spicy tomato gravy
chana pulao	spicy rice dish with chickpeas
chapatti	flat north Indian wheat bread cooked on a **tawa**
chole	white chickpeas
chopsuey	stir-fried vegetables on a bed of deep-fried noodles
chowmein	stir-fried Chinese noodles containing vegetables and/or meat and eggs
chutney	piquant side dish made with fruit or vegetables in a base of oil and spices
cumin	spice commonly used in Indian cooking; either whole seeds or ground cumin can be used
dahi	plain yoghurt; also known as natural yoghurt or curd; used as a curry ingredient or as a base for **raita**
dahi vada	deep-fried snack served with yoghurt
dal	any lentil or pulse, including dried peas and beans; generic name for any lentil curry
dal makhni	lentil dish with melted butter
dal tadka	lentil dish with cumin and mustard seeds
davara	stainless steel container for cooling down hot coffee or tea; used only in south Indian eateries
dhaba	roadside eatery along highways
dosa	crisp pancake made from rice and **dal** batter; can be eaten plain or with **masala**
drumstick	vegetable native to India; looks like a squash, only longer and thinner
fenugreek	strong aromatic spice native to India; ground fenugreek is an essential item in curry powder
fruit chaat	pieces of fruit laced with lemon and pepper
gajar halwa	carrot fudge
garam masala	specific blend of spices — usually cardamom, coriander, cinnamon, black cumin, mace, nutmeg, cloves and pepper — in paste or powder form
ghee	clarified butter or pure butter fat where milk solids have been removed
gingelly oil	sesame seed oil
gobi	cauliflower
golgappa	north Indian snack filled with chickpeas and potatoes
gulab jamun	north Indian dessert of deep-fried milk balls soaked in sugar syrup
halwa	fudge; popular dessert in north and south India

idli	steamed south Indian rice cake made from rice and **urad dal**
imli	tamarind; also known as Indian date; tamarind juice or paste acts as a souring agent
jaggery	coarse, unrefined sugar from the juice of crushed sugar cane; a typical sweetening agent in Indian desserts and sweets; gives an earthy flavour
jal jeera	tangy drink made with cumin seeds, mint leaves and coriander leaves
jalebi	sweet deep-fried snack made from flour
jeera	cumin seeds or powder
kadhai	round shaped cooking utensil similar to a wok
kadhai paneer	vegetable dish consisting of cottage cheese and capsicum; served in a **kadhai**
kadi	any thick yoghurt-based gravy
kadi kofta	fried gram flour balls in yoghurt-based gravy
kala chana	black chickpeas
kalonji	commonly known as Nigella or black onion seeds; imparts a peppery flavour
kari	Tamil word for 'sauce'; known today in the English speaking world as 'curry'
kebab	small pieces of grilled meat on a skewer
keema	minced meat
keema naan	north Indian bread filled with minced mutton
kesri halwa	fudge made with saffron
khameer	baker's yeast
kheer	north Indian rice pudding
khullad	clay mugs in which tea is served; often used by vendors in railway stations
kofta	vegetables or meat shaped into balls
kulcha	north Indian flour bread baked in the **tandoor** and eaten with chickpeas
kulfi	Indian ice cream made with milk, almonds and **pista**
laddu	ball-shaped sweet dessert made from **besan** and served in sugar syrup
lassi	yoghurt and milk drink; also known in Delhi as the Yoghurt Cooler
maida	plain flour or all-purpose flour
makhni	melted butter
malai	name given to any concentrated and aromatic gravy used as a base for **kofta**; also the cream that develops when milk is boiled
malai kofta	deep-fried patties of minced vegetables in rich gravy

masala	blend of spices and seasonings in a paste or powder form; also refers to any mixture that is used as a filling for **dosa**
masoor dal	red lentil
matka	earthen pitcher
matar	green peas
matar paneer	vegetarian dish of green peas and cottage cheese
matar pulao	rice dish cooked with green peas
matti	round-shaped deep-fried biscuit made of **besan**; sold mainly by **chai walas**
mausambi	sweet lime; the juice is also squeezed and taken as an appetiser
meeta paan	sweet betel
methi	another name for **fenugreek**
milagu thanni	pepper water; known in the English speaking world as 'mulligatawny soup'
missi roti	north Indian barley bread
moong dal	green gram **dal**; also known as split mung beans
momos	popular steamed or fried Tibetan rice snack
mooli	radish
mooli paratha	unleavened wheat bread filled with radish
Mughlai	non-vegetarian food introduced by the Mughals
murgh	chicken
murgh tandoori	chicken cooked in a **tandoor**
mustard seeds	brownish-black seeds usually tempered in hot oil to bring out its nutty flavour
naan	north Indian flour bread made in the **tandoor**; contains yeast; can be plain or filled with garlic or minced mutton
nav rattan pulao	rice dish cooked during Mughal times; originally prepared with nine major ingredients
Navrata	Hindu religious festival
paan	betel leaf cultivated in India; also the name of the delicacy that Indians chew after meals
paan wala	person who sells **paan** on the streets
palak	spinach; also known as saag in north India
palak paneer	vegetable dish comprising spinach and cottage cheese
paneer	cottage cheese
paneer makhni	dish consisting of cottage cheese and melted butter
paneer tikka	cubes of cottage cheese cooked in a **tandoor**
paratha	multi-layered unleavened north Indian wheat bread; comes either plain or with filling

papad (pappadam)	deep-fried crispy crackers made from **urad dal**; known as pappadam in south India
papdi	deep-fried flour discs served with mango chutney, mint chutney and yoghurt
payasam	thick, creamy south Indian dessert made from rice and milk, and flavoured with spices
phaluda	macaroni type vermicelli
phulka	another name for **chapatti**
pista	pistachios
pongal	rice based south Indian breakfast dish; also the name of a south Indian festival that celebrates the harvest
pudina	mint
pudina paratha	unleavened wheat bread with mint paste
pulao	rice dish cooked with vegetables, spices and yoghurt
puri	fluffy south Indian wheat flour pancake
raita	yoghurt accompaniment for rice or bread; may be plain or contain vegetables or fruit
rasam	light, watery, tangy soup from south India; taken with rice (south India) or as an appetiser (north India)
rawa	semolina, a coarse grain that comes from durum wheat
rawa payasam	**payasam** made from semolina
rogan josh	Kashmiri lamb curry
roti	generic name for all breads made in north India; also the name of a popular variety of unleavened bread
rumali roti	very thin north Indian flat bread
saada paan	simple betel
sabudana	sago
sabudana kheer	pudding made from sago beans
saffron	expensive orange coloured flavouring from the stigma of the *crocus sativus*; gives a delicate but distinct honey-like taste
sambar	south Indian stew made from lentils and vegetables, and flavoured with tamarind
samosa	north Indian deep-fried snack with savoury filling
saunf	aniseed; eaten at the end of a meal to aid digestion
seek kebab	minced mutton kebabs grilled over a charcoal fire
semiya	vermicelli
semiya payasam	**payasam** made from vermicelli
sevaien kheer	pudding made from wheat flour vermicelli

shahi paneer	cottage cheese in rich gravy; named after the emperor Shah Jahan
shakra pongal	south Indian rice-based dessert
shammi kebab	mutton and lentil kebabs
shrikhand	north Indian dessert made from yoghurt and **jaggery**
suji halwa	semolina fudge
tandoor	traditional clay oven fired by heat from charcoal; used for cooking tandoori meats and **naan**
tandoori roti	north Indian wheat bread cooked in the **tandoor**
tawa	flat cast iron griddle used for cooking **dosa**, **paratha** and **chapatti**
tawa ki roti	north Indian wheat bread cooked on a **tawa**; also known as **chapatti**
thali	south Indian rice meal served in a stainless steel rimmed plate
tikka	cubes (of chicken, mutton or cottage cheese)
tikki	cake
turmeric	important spice and colouring agent in Indian cooking; comes from the root of a ginger-like plant
uppuma	south Indian dish made from semolina
uthampam	south Indian pancake made from **dosa** batter; cooked with condiments such as tomatoes, chillies and onion
urad dal	black gram lentil
vada	south Indian crispy, deep-fried doughnut made from lentils

DELHI CUISINE

Indian cuisine is vast, complex and varied, as varied as the many languages and dialects that are spoken throughout the subcontinent. Just as each state or province in India has its own social customs, language and culture, so it is with food. In fact, it is not unusual to find the same dish cooked differently within a region. There is probably no single way of defining Indian cuisine. Outside the country, though, most people would recognise Indian cuisine by some select dishes and its heavy reliance on spices.

Indian cuisine can be broadly divided into north Indian and south Indian, and further categorised into vegetarian and non-vegetarian. The latter term might seem strange, but it simply means food that contains meat.

North Indian cuisine is based on *atta* flour, from which unleavened bread such as chapatti and roti are made (these are the staple flat breads of people living in the north). South Indian food, on the other hand, revolves around rice and is relatively light on the stomach. This is their main and essential difference. Both, however, rely heavily on a wide variety of pulses and lentils for their protein. Pulses include chickpeas, red kidney beans and black-eyed beans. Among the lentils are *chana* dal, *urad* dal, *masoor* dal, *arhar* dal and *moong* dal.

Because of the dominant influence of Hinduism, vegetarian food is the mainstay of a large section of the Indian population. Yet India is also home to some of the world's finest mouth-watering, non-vegetarian cuisine that centres around chicken and mutton. The advent of Mughal kingdoms in this Hindu-dominated country brought in its wake a cuisine that was both delicious and spicy and which left an indelible mark on Indian cooking as a whole.

Be it vegetarian or non-vegetarian, from the north or the south, Indian cuisine is a great mix of exotic spices, age-old herbs, cereals and dried fruit that provide a spectacular variety of nutritious and aromatic dishes. In recent years, the physical boundaries that used to separate north and south Indian cuisine has all but disappeared and one can enjoy all the varieties of Indian food no matter where in India one happens to be.

Then there are the spices, the heart and soul of Indian cuisine. Their use not only varies from region to region, they are combined differently. The most commonly used spices are pepper, mustard, cumin, asafoetida, coriander, turmeric, chillies and ginger. Adding to the aromas and flavours are bay leaf, sesame, fenugreek, cinnamon, cardamom, cloves and saffron, an expensive flavouring that comes from the stigmas of a crocus which blooms for only two weeks a year.

Indian cuisine is unique in the sense that most dishes cannot be eaten in isolation. It is not possible, for example, to have a north Indian bread such as chapatti, roti or naan on its own. Bread is meant to be eaten with side dishes, either a vegetarian or non-vegetarian gravy-based dish. The same goes for rice, unless the rice you order is a pulao or biryani, which already has a mix of vegetables or meat in it.

One thing is for sure. Whether you are biting into a piece of tandoori chicken or having a south Indian rice meal, you will leave wanting more.

BEEF AND PORK

For religious reasons, Hindus do not eat beef because they consider the cow a sacred animal (even global food chains in India do not serve beef) and Muslims avoid pork. But such is the eclecticism in Indian food habits that communities in the country's tribal and Christian-dominated north-east happily consume beef. Where meat is served, expect mutton, chicken or beef. Even then, such places would often choose not to serve meat especially on special festival or religious days. Seafood is the mainstay for many communities along the coast, both because it is cheap and can be sourced easily.

Paan — an Indian del(h)icacy

If there is anything in India that is as popular as the country's varied cuisine, it is the ubiquitous paan. Paan is the Hindi word for the sub-continental chew, which Indians have been consuming for centuries. For many of them, chewing paan is a national pastime and offering one after a meal is considered common courtesy.

This unusual after-dinner treat is sold on almost every street corner and is available in many varieties. It is also served at weddings and banquets. Besides possessing medicinal and digestive properties, it is said to act as a mouth freshener. In Delhi, paan *walas* do brisk business every night as people flock to them after a hearty dinner.

Paan gets its name from a heart-shaped betel leaf that is specially cultivated all over the country. There are three broad varieties of leaf — the south Indian variety, the Bengal paan and the Benaras paan (from that Hindu holy city along the Ganges River). Such is the demand for the Indian betel leaf in neighbouring Pakistan that it figures high on the list of smuggled items!

Preparing a paan is simple. The leaf is first cleaned with water and dried. It is then covered with a thin layer of lime paste. In north India, paan sellers then spread red-coloured syrup (extracted from a native plant) over the lime paste. The betel leaf is usually not eaten plain, although some elderly people tend to do that.

Depending on one's fancy, buyers have a choice of either *meeta* (sweet) paan or *saada* (simple) paan. In *meeta* paan, the leaf is filled with a sprinkling of ingredients such as cardamom, mint, anise, jellied fruit, grated coconut, areca nut and honey. The leaf is then folded into a neat triangle and sometimes fastened with a clove. In *saada* paan, the only ingredients are lime paste and syrup although tobacco will be added if requested. Note that experts have warned that regular consumption of paan with tobacco can cause mouth cancer. People who eat *meeta* paan swallow the entire leaf and its contents while those chewing the *saada* paan would mostly spit out the fibrous core of the leaf.

If you are game to try paan, go for the *meeta* paan first as the sweetness will make it more palatable. Be warned though that your lips will be stained red because of the syrup. On the street, a paan would cost between Rs.3 and Rs.8. If you are not adventurous enough, visit a paan *wala* in the evening and see him in action! First timers might find the idea of eating paan daunting, but it is something worth trying… at least once!

PAAN — A SYMBOL OF LOVE?

Many Indians believe that paan is also an aphrodisiac. In olden times, a woman who wanted to bed a man would offer him a paan or invite him to have one. Thus only married men and women were expected to consume paan. In some Hindu marriage ceremonies today, the bride would hold the betel roll in her mouth and wait for the groom to take a bite on the protruding end.

Silver foil and Indian sweets

The visitor to India may find this fact difficult to believe, but up to 15 million tonnes of pure silver is turned into edible silver foil every year! This is prepared with great caution — heavy equipment is used to beat small balls of silver into paper-thin sheets. Indeed, they are so thin that they break up when touched with the hands. Silver foil has no aroma or taste and is used to garnish mainly sweets and sweet dishes. It is sold between sheets of tissue paper or small pieces of newspaper. A visit to any Indian sweet shop will reveal the extent to which silver foil is used to embellish sweets.

Chai — Delhi's official drink

There is probably no street in Delhi where one cannot find a chai *wala*. He is the ubiquitous tea vendor who is, more often than not, a one-man industry serving hundreds of cups of tea to Indians who cannot survive without the brew that the English introduced to the country. Most of the tea that Indians drink comes from Assam and Darjeeling in the northeast.

Although tea bags are becoming increasingly popular, Delhites — as the people in the city call themselves — relish the brew most when it is made by boiling tea leaves in hot water. Street vendors serve tea, almost always with milk and sugar, in small china cups or throwaway plastic cups. In many railway stations, environmentally-friendly clay mugs called *khullad* are used.

For tea with a difference, ask for cardamom tea or ginger tea. Cardamom tea is tea that has been infused with cardamom and some cloves; these spices give it a distinctive flavour. Tea infused with ginger is believed to have its own medicinal value. Most tea vendors tend to put a lot of sugar as a matter of habit, so forewarn them if you want less sugar in your cup.

Enterprising chai *walas* offer more than just tea. They also sell tidbits such as *matti* and bread *pakoda*, which go perfectly well with the piping hot sweet brew. During Delhi's winter, it will be difficult to see an idle chai *wala*!

North
Indian cuisine

Appetisers

A typical Indian meal traditionally begins with an appetiser, which serves to enhance appetite and prepare the senses for the meal that is to come. These days, though, many Indians prefer to skip it and plunge straight into the main meal. One common appetiser is fruit juice. On the streets, vendors use electrical juicers or hand operated mechanical devices to extract the juices of oranges and lime, which they then sell for an incredible Rs.10! Lime juice is served with either water or soda, to which salt or sugar can be added on request. Juice is served chilled during Delhi's scorching summer months when temperatures can go up to 40° Celsius. During winter most people prefer their juice to be at room temperature.

Mausambi juice

The juice of the *mausambi* fruit, otherwise known as sweet lime, makes another refreshing appetiser. This green citrus fruit resembles the orange in size and shape. Amazingly, its cream-coloured flesh tastes both sweet and sour. Being rich in calories (35 to 45 calories per 100 grams), two glasses of this energising drink is said to be able to sustain a person for almost the whole day. If you want to try *mausambi* juice, head for the streets. It is not sold in Delhi's supermarkets or convenience stores. Take it plain or as the Indians do, with a sprinkling of black pepper.

Jal jeera

Jal jeera or 'cumin seed water' is to north India what lemonade is to America. This tangy drink contains *jeera*, or cumin seeds, the paste of mint leaves and coriander leaves, dried mango powder, black salt (rock salt mined from soft stone quarries along the Ganges River), lemon juice and a pinch of sugar. Optional condiments are *imli* (tamarind), green chillies and ginger. All these are thoroughly mixed; cold water is then added to the concoction. Whole mint leaves are sprinkled last. In the blistering heat of summer, *Jal jeera* is sold on the streets in earthen pitchers called *matkas*. If you are trying this drink for the first time, take a sip first; many newcomers to India have been taken aback by its sharp taste. *Jal jeera* also works as a digestive aid and is especially good after oily food or a heavy meal.

Lassi

Lassi, which looks very much like a milk shake or smoothie, is the name given to a yoghurt drink. Not only is it very easy to prepare (simply blend yoghurt until it froths at the top) and a great thirst quencher in summer, the good bacteria in the yoghurt makes it an excellent digestive aid. If you are keen to try lassi, it is best that you get it from a restaurant and not from street vendors, where hygiene is suspect. Lassi tastes bland and you can ask for salt or sugar to be added. Some eateries go the extra mile and sprinkle dried mint leaves or rose water to give the drink a

relaxing fragrance. Although lassi is a popular appetiser, it is not available in supermarkets or convenience stores. In Delhi, lassi is often called the 'Yoghurt Cooler'.

Papad

Papads are roasted or deep-fried crunchy crackers made from *urad* dal, or black gram lentil. They come either plain or flavoured with spices such as cumin seeds and black peppercorns. Delhi restaurants serving north Indian food almost always offer the flavoured ones together with mint chutney as an accompaniment. Although

papad is seen as an appetiser, many Delhites choose to also have them with the main meal. You can buy pre-cooked papad in packets — these come as thin, dry, round cakes — and fry them in oil at home (see how they swell and curl in the hot oil). For a healthier version, roast them in an oven toaster. On the streets, vendors sprinkle black pepper on cooked papad to intensify the taste.

Soup

Soup is not an integral part of traditional Indian meals. About the only indigenous Indian soup is *milagu thanni*, or mulligatawny soup, which hails from south India. However, with the growing demand for Chinese food in the past 20 years, the popularity of soup has taken off so much that drinking soup has become part and parcel of the Indian urban dining experience.

In Delhi, soup is easily available at high-end restaurants, in small shops tucked away in busy markets as well as from mobile vans converted into mini kitchens. Many families make soup at home but this would not be done on a regular basis. Locally manufactured ready-to-make soup, which involve just heating and serving, is sold in Indian convenience stores for between Rs.3 and Rs.10 and is gaining popularity. Even then, Indians who like soup do not have it every day. Soup continues to remain very much a feature of eating out. Where soup is served they stand out markedly in taste, thanks to the use of spices, chillies, ginger and garlic.

Mulligatawny soup

This soup has its origins in south India where it is known as *milagu thanni*, or pepper water. The Tamil name was adapated by the British during the colonial era and transformed to 'mulligatawny'. Although this soup is not easily available in Delhi, it makes a very nice appetiser for any meal. This lightly-spiced soup, which is always served hot, is made with lentils, onion, grated ginger, garam masala, dried red pepper, coriander powder, black pepper, chopped carrots, dried tomatoes, vegetable stock, lemon, coconut milk and coriander leaves. There are minor variations; some eateries add a small quantity of cooked white rice to it while chicken is included in non-vegetarian places.

Creamy tomato soup

This vegetarian soup is flavoured with herbs such as basil and coriander leaves and lightly spiced with cinnamon, cloves and black pepper. Made from fresh or canned tomatoes and the liberal use of cream and butter, it is very popular during Delhi's winter when it is served with croutons or bread sticks.

Creamy mushroom soup

Mushroom is not a popular ingredient in Indian cuisine and as such, mushroom soup is not as sought after as, say, tomato or chicken soup. Yet, it has plenty of takers wherever it is offered. Small pieces of button mushroom are simmered together

with chopped onion, tomatoes, seasonal vegetables, butter or ghee and *maida*, or all-purpose flour. It is then seasoned with black pepper and salt. Milk is added to make the soup smooth and creamy. Some restaurants add cumin, cloves and *pudina*, or mint, for extra flavour. This filling soup has a sharp and spicy taste.

Mixed vegetable soup

Containing lots of vegetables, this soup is always a winner with the people of Delhi. Carrots, green peas, tomatoes, potatoes, turnip and onion are chopped into small pieces and fried in butter together with ginger-garlic paste (sometimes mustard seeds are added at this stage) and then left to simmer. The broth is flavoured with bay leaves, black pepper and the usual spices such as cumin powder and cloves. When ready to be served, coriander leaves are thrown in as garnish.

Hot and sour vegetable soup

This thick broth consists of vegetables such as ribbed gourd, capsicum, carrots, beans, cauliflower, cabbage and spinach. Seasoned with soya sauce and spices and thickened with cornflour, its sour taste comes from the addition of lemon juice. This soup is also prepared in many of the city's Chinese eateries.

Sweet corn soup/sweet corn chicken soup

This wholesome and nutritious soup consists of tender corn kernels, which have been pressure-cooked and then roughly ground. Sugar, salt, soya sauce, chilli sauce and vinegar give the soup its distinctive flavour. This soup is a fusion of Indian and Chinese as can be seen from the use of soya sauce. It is served hot along with a sprinkling of  cooked corn kernels. In non-vegetarian restaurants, chicken meat that has been coated with cream or butter is added to make the soup more robust. Green chillies are thrown in to give a stronger flavour.

Chicken soup/clear chicken soup

Chicken soup is another popular soup in Delhi. With shredded chicken, finely sliced carrots and cabbage, spices and Indian herbs, this soup is distinctly tasty. All these ingredients are cooked together in chicken stock and cornflour until the soup thickens. Another popular variation of this soup is clear chicken soup, which is simply a more watered-down version. Both soups are garnished with coriander leaves.

Rice

Rice is the staple food for millions of people in India. It is a unique vehicle for bringing out the flavours of accompanying dishes. The best variety of rice is Basmati rice; this long grained rice is always used in high-end restaurants and on special occasions such as weddings. Wherever you go in Delhi, steamed white rice is always available and you would eat this together with side dishes of meat or vegetables.

In this city, too, you will find two other special preparations of rice: pulao and biryani. Pulao is essentially rice steamed and cooked together with diced vegetables and yoghurt. It is lightly spiced with cumin and coriander. Biryani, on the other hand, is a meat-based dish; chicken and mutton are the usual choices. The meat is first cooked partially and separately with spices and then transferred to the rice pot where the cooking process is completed. Between the two, biryani is heavier and spicier. Whichever you choose to have, these rice dishes are best eaten with raita or chutney.

Chana pulao

For a hot and spicy pulao, try *chana pulao* (chickpea rice) with its liberal use of green chillies and cloves. *Chana*, or chickpeas, are first soaked in water. When they are soft enough, they are added to the rice together with some cottage cheese, or paneer as it is known in Delhi. The whole concoction is cooked together with chopped onion, tomatoes, green chillies, cloves, cardamom, coriander leaves and mint leaves. The inclusion of cottage cheese often gives the impression of the presence of eggs in this vegetarian dish. Some cooks add synthetic yellow and green food colouring to the rice.

Matar pulao

The main ingredient in this nourishing dish is *matar*, or green peas. The dish is simply flavoured with only cumin seeds, cloves, pepper and garlic. Even though it is neither hot nor spicy, some Indians consider it the best rice dish ever, better than even the highly rated biryani. This tasty and satisfying dish is commonly prepared in Indian homes.

Vegetable pulao

With a wonderful aroma and a colourful presentation, this dish is a feast for the senses. Here, the rice is prepared in a base of light spices and some yoghurt and cooked together with diced vegetables such as capsicum, carrots, gourd, pumpkin, beans, potatoes and coriander leaves. Vegetable pulao is satisfying enough to fill the stomach yet light enough to be easily digested.

Nav rattan pulao

It is said that the Mughal emperor Akbar gave the name *Nav Rattans*, meaning Nine Jewels, to nine of his most valued ministers. Considered the jewel of all pulao dishes, connoisseurs say this heritage dish originally comprised nine main ingredients. Today, though, more than nine ingredients go into its making; these include yoghurt, cottage cheese, peas, cauliflower, cherries, carrots, cashew nuts, raisins, lemon, onion, garam masala, chilli powder, green chillies, mint leaves, coriander leaves and garlic paste. The rice is usually a vibrant orange due to the use of saffron; some eateries in Old Delhi add other permitted colourings to make the dish more appealing. In some places, the dish is topped with hard-boiled eggs.

Mutton biryani

This dish is another legacy of the Mughals. It is not an exaggeration to say that it is the mother of all non-vegetarian north Indian dishes. With chopped mutton pieces marinated in strong spices and then cooked together with almonds, cashew nuts, raisins, cinnamon, cardamom and saffron dissolved in milk, it has an inviting and irresistible aroma. As is the case with biryani dishes, the rice and meat are cooked together in a large metal pot or pressure cooker.

Egg fried rice

This is the Indian equivalent of the Chinese *yong chow* fried rice. Here, steamed rice is mixed with pieces of hard-boiled eggs and other condiments such as finely chopped green chillies, cloves, cinnamon, cardamom, white pepper, chopped coriander leaves, as well as finely
sliced onion and ginger. The inclusion of eggs into the rice makes this dish different from all other rice dishes.

Vegetable fried rice

If you want a rice dish chockfull of vegetables, this is it. Vegetables such as potatoes, carrots, beans, green peas and green bell peppers are stir-fried together with cooked rice in some ghee. Cashew nuts, cloves, garam masala, chilli powder, cinnamon powder and salt provide extra flavour. Most people in Delhi will have raita on the side. Some eateries will top the dish with a thin layer of paneer (see white strips in the photograph below).

Bread

Bread or roti is an integral part of the diet of the people in north India and is a ready source of carbohydrate and fibre. As well as being the generic name for bread, roti is also the name given to a popular variety of unleavened bread that is made in the north. Other typical north Indian breads are naan and paratha, which together with roti are invariably eaten with gravy dishes.

Naan is the name given to the tandoor-baked bread from Punjab. Mostly triangular in shape, it is thicker and fluffier than roti because it has *khameer*, or baker's yeast, in it. Apart from yeast, other ingredients for making the dough include *maida*, salt, milk, yoghurt, ghee, poppy seeds and nigella (black onion seeds).

Paratha refers to a yeast-free bread that is shallow-fried in either ghee or vegetable oil on a cast iron griddle called *tawa*, which is heated from below. The main ingredients are *atta*, water and salt to taste. Some people may add egg to the dough. Paratha comes either plain or stuffed with fillings such as potatoes, lentils, vegetables, eggs or cottage cheese.

Tandoori roti

Of the many varieties of north Indian bread, this whole wheat bread is undoubtedly the most popular, partly also because it is the cheapest! It is prepared with *atta* flour, some *maida*, water and salt. When the dough is ready it is

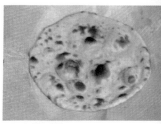

portioned into smaller pieces. Each piece is flattened into a circular shape and then placed in the tandoor. *Tandoori roti* is best eaten hot when dipped in a gravy-based dish; when cold, it hardens and is tougher to chew.

Tawa ki roti (chapatti)

Also known as chapatti, this thin flat bread is made from *atta* flour and cooked on a *tawa*. Chapatti need not be eaten warm. As this bread is rather dry, it is best eaten with a gravy-based dish.

Rumali roti

This is the bread of choice when it comes to Mughlai dishes such as chicken curry or mutton curry. Most people use *atta* flour although some may substitute it with *maida*. It can be prepared either on a *tawa* or on an electric or gas cooking range. Because the dough is stretched many times over, this bread is bigger and thinner than chapatti. In fact, it can be as thin as a handkerchief, a quality which makes it very easy to chew.

THE TANDOOR

When it comes to cooking, one of India's greatest inventions is the tandoor. This is a large, circular clay oven — about 1.5 metres high — heated from the bottom by charcoal. You may call it the Indian barbeque. The heat from the charcoal warms up the sides of the oven, evenly cooking the bread dough that has been pressed onto its inside walls with a small, thick wad of cloth. When the bread is ready, it is retrieved with a pair of sharp iron rods. In addition to bread, the tandoor is indispensable in the preparation of Mughlai mutton and chicken dishes. The good thing about the tandoor is that very little oil is needed. At home, the easiest substitute for the clay oven would be a coal barbeque grill.

Missi roti

Missi roti hails from the region of Punjab. It is slightly thicker than chapatti and can be cooked either on a *tawa* or in a tandoor. The main ingredients are *atta* and gram flour, oil or ghee, barley, dry fenugreek leaves, cumin seeds, asafoetida and a dash of turmeric, which gives it a bright yellow colour. When freshly cooked, this bread is as crisp as a biscuit. It goes well with vegetarian dishes, particularly those with spinach and cottage cheese.

Plain naan/butter naan

As the name implies, plain naan comes without any toppings or fillings. This tandoor-baked bread is most delicious when eaten with dal, or lentil, gravy. Try butter naan if you want naan with a little more flavour.

Garlic naan

Here, garlic is a key ingredient. Minced garlic is mixed into the dough, which is then shaped and placed in the tandoor. When the bread is ready, more garlic may be added, this time in the form of raw garlic paste. To the Indians, garlic is a powerful medicinal herb that not only enhances the immune system but also helps lower high blood pressure, thus reducing the risk of heart disease. Depending on the potency of the raw garlic, garlic naan can taste quite fiery.

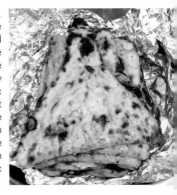

Keema naan

Keema means 'mincemeat' and minced mutton is the identifying ingredient in this speciality. Here, mutton that has been pre-cooked with spices — cloves, garam masala, cardamom and cinnamon — is stuffed into the dough, which then goes into the tandoor. *Keema naan* is served sizzling hot with side dishes of yoghurt, chutney or a gravy-based curry.

Aloo paratha

This type of bread contains *aloo*, or potato, which has been boiled and mashed. In my opinion, potato makes the best stuffing for paratha. Thoroughly mixed into the potato are onion, green chillies, coriander leaves, red pepper, garam masala, lemon juice, pomegranate seeds and coriander seeds. This mixture is then thrown on the dough as it is being cooked on the *tawa*. This bread makes a perfect meal with any seasonal vegetable dish or chutney.

Mooli paratha

After *aloo paratha*, this is the next most popular paratha. It is filled with *mooli*, or radish, a root vegetable that is reputed to possess many medicinal properties, among them the ability to treat coughs and sinusitis. Indian apothecaries advise people with Hepatitis to consume as much radish as possible and prescribe drinking the juice of radish leaves.

Vegetable paratha

Vegetable paratha contains a mixture of chopped seasonal vegetables such as spinach, turnip, cauliflower, cabbage and capsicum, flavoured with garam masala, cloves, cinnamon and red chilli powder. Chopped green chillies and coriander leaves add to the flavour.

Pudina paratha

Pudina is the north Indian word for 'mint', an herb that practitioners of Indian medicine use to treat digestive disorders. The mint makes this the most aromatic of all parathas. Although the use of oil and ghee suggests the dish is heavy and hence more difficult to digest, the mint provides the perfect counterbalance and its health benefits surpasses any concern the oil or ghee might bring.

Puri

This deep-fried wheat flour pancake is yet another popular north Indian bread. Puri is most often eaten at breakfast with either chickpeas or a gravy dish of potatoes and onion. An interesting effect takes place when the dough is put into hot oil — they fill up with steam and balloon within seconds. They remain inflated when served immediately and deflates when broken. Depending on their size, it is possible to eat as many as six pieces at one meal.

Bhatura

Bhatura is a soft, crisp bread that is deep-fried in ghee. The dough is plain leavened flour mixed with yoghurt (sometimes, an egg might be broken into the dough) and seasoned with salt and sugar. Popular as a breakfast dish, it is often eaten with a side dish of chickpeas.

Kulcha

Kulcha, which originates from Punjab, is somewhat like *bhatura* except that it is not deep-fried. Rather, it is baked in a tandoor or electric oven with some ghee or oil rubbed on the dough. The ingredients include *atta*, warm milk and yeast. The bread is eaten with a dish of chickpeas. The result is a light yet nutritious meal.

WHAT IS A CURRY?

The word 'curry' comes from the Tamil word *kari*, which means 'sauce'. In India, a curry can consist of meat (chicken or mutton), seafood (fish or prawns) or vegetables. These are cooked together with a variety of spices and left to simmer in a liquid, usually a mix of water, yoghurt or cream. In the south, coconut milk is often added to make the sauce.

Vegetarian

What sets Indian cuisine apart from the others is the sheer variety of vegetarian food on offer. In a country where millions of people do not eat meat for religious reasons, the very large number of vegetarian dishes that India churns out never ceases to amaze. Apart from vegetables such as cabbage, capsicum, carrots, cauliflower, gourd, radish and tomato, other main ingredients are lentils (of which there is a wide variety) and paneer (cottage cheese). Here are some of the main north Indian vegetarian dishes that you can try in Delhi as you tuck into bread and rice!

Dal makhni

This is by far the most popular north Indian vegetarian dish. Its popularity has to do with the fact that it goes perfectly with bread and rice, even plain rice. The key ingredients are black gram, Bengal gram and kidney beans; these are soaked in water for up to eight hours and then pressure-cooked. The dish is flavoured with green chillies, cumin seeds, pepper, cloves and garlic. Different chefs would prepare the dish in their own way, but it tastes great no matter how it is done. The secret of this dish likes in the *makhni*, or melted butter, which is poured over the dish just before it is served.

Dal tadka

This is yet another popular lentil dish that comes from the Punjab region. *Moong* dal, or green gram, is first pressure-cooked with some turmeric. Separately, cumin and mustard seeds are fried in ghee until they splutter ('*tadka*' refers to the spluttering effect) and then asafoetida is added. When the

lentils are ready, green chillies, garlic, curry leaves and coriander leaves are added. The cumin and mustard seeds are mixed in last. *Dal tadka* goes very well with bread.

Chana masala

This age-old recipe also comes from Punjab. *Chana*, or chickpeas, are traditionally soaked overnight and cooked in thick tomato gravy. Some restaurants use canned chickpeas for convenience. Flavouring the gravy are a blend of the potent

garam masala, turmeric, coriander powder, crushed ginger, onion, tomatoes and chillies, both green and red. This dish is a perfect complement to breads and steamed white rice.

Palak paneer

A Punjabi culinary delight and my all-time favourite, *palak paneer* is a combination of tender spinach leaves and finely cut cubes of cottage cheese cooked to perfection in oil. Other ingredients include onion, tomatoes, ginger, garlic, bay leaves and cumin seeds. It is the perfect dish to have with roti, chapatti or naan, as well as steamed rice. Some restaurants, however, tend to use a little more oil than necessary. Caution them if that is not how you want it done.

COTTAGE CHEESE

Apart from yoghurt, north Indian cuisine stands out for its use of paneer, which is a mild white cheese made from low fat cow's milk. Paneer is also widely consumed in neighbouring Pakistan and Nepal. Unlike other types of cheese, the Indian cottage cheese does not melt when heated and as such, can be cubed and cooked in curry dishes, both vegetarian and non-vegetarian. A 100-gram piece of paneer is said to give 265 calories of energy, 18.3 grams of protein and 1.2 grams of carbohydrate; it is no wonder that many people in India consider it a good substitute for meat.

Kadhai paneer

The word *kadhai* comes from the Mughal kitchen and refers to a round-shaped cooking utensil that looks very much like a Chinese wok. *Kadhai paneer* is a thick gravy dish comprising cottage cheese and capsicum. The gravy is prepared with onions and tomatoes and flavoured with a variety of spices. When ready to be eaten, the dish is served in a small *kadhai* and placed in the centre of the table for everyone to tuck in.

Shahi paneer

This dish of cottage cheese, which comes in rich gravy, was once the favourite of Mughal emperor Shah Jahan. The chefs of his court would lovingly prepare the dish with as many as 32 spices. Today, those 32 spices are reduced to mainly garam masala, powdered pepper, *kalonji*, *ajwain*, cardamom and turmeric. Other condiments include onion, ginger and garlic. Before the dish is served, it would be sprinkled with a mix of nuts such as almonds, cashew nuts, walnuts and *pista*.

Matar paneer

This popular gravy-based vegetarian dish from Punjab contains peas and cottage cheese. Here, pieces of cubed paneer are fried until they turn golden brown and then put aside. The gravy is made separately with chopped onion and ginger, whey, coriander, turmeric and minced tomatoes, and seasoned with salt and pepper. The cheese cubes and *matar*, or green peas, are then added to the gravy and cooked for a short while.

Paneer makhni

Containing both butter and cubes of cottage cheese, *paneer makhni* is a very rich dish. Butter and oil are first heated in a pan, to which onion and ginger-garlic paste are added. Turmeric, chilli powder and tomato puree then follow and these are cooked until the oil separates. Milk, salt, sugar and paneer cubes are then added and the dish is left to simmer for another two minutes.

Paneer tikka

This is truly a north Indian delicacy and one that can be quite filling! If you like cottage cheese, do not miss the lightly charred cubes (*tikka*) marinated in a blend of spices. The cottage cheese is usually cooked in the tandoor but it can be done quite well on a barbeque grill, too. If dipped in mint sauce, *paneer tikka* can be taken as a starter. A glass of chilled beer rounds the meal off perfectly.

Paneer roll/paneer egg roll

If you have time for only a quick lunch, having a few paneer rolls will stand you in good stead. Each roll is filled with a delicious mixture of paneer, boiled potatoes, grated onion and garlic. The batter for the roll is made from *atta*, *maida*, milk and butter, and

seasoned with black pepper and salt. When the batter is of the right consistency, it is poured on to a *tawa* and turned over when it begins to bubble and puff up. When the roll is ready, it is filled with the mixture and then neatly rolled up. Paneer rolls can be heated up in the microwave oven before being served. In the case of paneer egg roll, a beaten egg would be added to the batter.

Aloo gobi

This is a simple dish consisting of diced potato and *gobi*, or cauliflower, cut into small florets. With a combination of spices such as garam masala, cumin seeds, cinnamon, ground pepper, *kalonji*, *ajwain*, garlic cloves and onion, *aloo gobi* is always a winner.

Stuffed capsicum

Stuffed vegetables have a following of their own especially in northern and central India. Indeed, cooked vegetables can become more palatable if they are stuffed with spices, ground ginger, onion and tomatoes. A whole capsicum is hollowed out and filled with cooked chopped onion, mashed potatoes, crumbled cottage cheese and red chillies. The stuffing is seasoned with tamarind, cumin seeds, turmeric, ginger, coriander and garam masala.

Stuffed aubergine

In this dish, aubergine (also known as brinjal) is first baked. Baking is preferred to frying as baking helps the vegetable retain its natural flavour. Without cutting off the stem, each aurbergine is then slit lengthwise into two or four segments. Some of the pulp is scooped out and replaced with stuffing consisting of coconut paste, spices, cashew nuts and tamarind. This is then cooked over low heat in some oil together with sliced onions, cloves, peppercorns and coriander. Some restaurants add baby potatoes to the dish.

Stuffed tomato/ stuffed bitter gourd

In both of these dishes, the vegetables are stuffed with chopped onion, diced carrots and potatoes, finely cut ginger, green chillies and coriander leaves, all of which have been flavoured with spices. Cubed paneer is sometimes added to the stuffing for the tomato dish; the cottage cheese is first dipped in a flour batter and then fried. While bitter gourd may not be as popular as eggplant or capsicum (perhaps because of its taste), it is prized for its medicinal properties. Rich in phosphorous and said to purify blood and activate the spleen and liver, bitter gourd is highly sought after by diabetic patients. It is also a purgative. The spices help take away much of the bitterness.

Mixed vegetables

The most common combination of vegetables in this dish are onion, tomatoes and capsicum. Optional ingredients include mushrooms and cottage cheese. All these are cut into fine pieces, marinated in oil, pepper powder and salt, and then grilled until they turn golden brown. Onion, turmeric, curry leaves, green chillies and grated coconut complete the dish.

Malai kofta

This is another popular north Indian dish. Koftas are the vegetable counterparts of minced meatballs. The vegetables are usually spinach, cabbage, cauliflower and potato. They are mashed, shaped into small balls and then deep fried. The word *malai* actually refers to 'milk cream' (or skimmed milk) as well as the concentrated and aromatic gravy that forms the base for the dish. Here, the gravy is made of onion, skimmed milk, ginger and garlic fried in vegetable oil and blended to make a paste. Koftas are an excellent accompaniment for rotis.

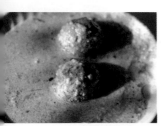

Kadi kofta

Kadi is the term given to any thick yoghurt-based curry. In this dish, the kofta is made from *besan*, or gram flour. The flour is seasoned with spices, shaped into balls, fried in some oil and then put aside. The gravy, which comprises a thin paste of gram flour and yogurt in equal proportions, is cooked separately. When the time is right, the flour balls are added to the gravy and simmered for a short while. *Kadi kofta* is a very soothing dish and goes well with both breads and rice.

Non-vegetarian

The origins of many north Indian meat dishes can be traced to the Mughal kitchens of the 16th and 17th centuries. The lavish attention that Mughal emperors heaped on their many fine monuments was only matched by their quest for culinary excellence, which has given rise to the rich and aromatic Mughlai cuisine that can be found not only in Delhi but all over the world. One enduring legacy of the Mughals is the practice of garnishing dishes with saffron, nuts and raisins. During the height of their power, Mughal rulers ate from dinnerware made of jade, silver and porcelain.

Chicken curry/mutton curry

Whether it is chicken or mutton curry, the spice base for both is quite similar, with the exception of green chillies, yoghurt and saffron for the latter. In these dishes, the meat is cut into small pieces and left to stew in the curry sauce until tender. These curries, which go very well with rice and breads, are undoubtedly two of the most popular Mughlai dishes.

Egg curry

Whichever way egg curry is cooked in India, it is a hearty dish and makes a perfect accompaniment to both rice dishes as well as breads, especially in the winter months. The rich gravy for this dish consists of tomatoes, onion, ginger and a range of spices and herbs including bay leaves, turmeric powder, cloves, cardamom, cinnamon, mustard seeds, poppy seeds and green and red chillies. The eggs in the curry are first hard-boiled and served either whole or cut into halves.

Chicken tikka/chicken tikka masala

Chicken tikka is boneless chicken cubes at its best and, depending on how hungry you are, you could have it as an appetiser or a main dish. Here, small chunks of cubed chicken — well marinated with crushed ginger and garlic, chilli powder, turmeric, salt, yoghurt, garam masala, lemon juice and coriander for a few hours — are placed on metal skewers and lowered into a tandoor where they are cooked to perfection (crispy on the outside, juicy on the inside). Some lemon juice and black pepper complete the taste.

The difference between chicken tikka and chicken tikka masala is that in the latter, the chicken is further cooked in a rich tomato-based gravy flavoured with ginger and spices. Some eateries add butter or cream to make the gravy richer.

A TRUE BRITISH NATIONAL DISH?

British Foreign Secretary Robin Cook once called chicken tikka masala 'a true British national dish', which many Indians (and Pakistanis) disagree! Its origin is said to have begun during the time of the British Raj — an Englishman insisted on having gravy with his chicken and the chef poured tomato sauce and some spices on the meat. That simple act unwittingly gave birth to a dish that, today, is a craze the world over.

Butter chicken

This chicken dish is one of Punjab's most famous. Like chicken tikka masala, it is a gravy-based dish that goes well with north Indian bread. The soul of this dish lies in its thick yet creamy gravy made from yoghurt, garam masala, onion, cumin seeds, powdered pepper, ginger, cloves and cinnamon with rich helpings of butter.

Kadhai chicken

This boneless chicken dish is both cooked and served in a *kadhai*, a small cooking utensil that looks like a wok. Cumin seeds, bay leaves and dried red chillies are first heated in oil. When the cumin begins to splutter, garam masala and onions are added and all the ingredients are sautéed for a few more minutes. The chicken pieces are then left to cook on low heat. The dish is garnished with coriander leaves and topped with a bit of butter.

Chicken do-pyaza

Do-pyaza means 'two onions'. Although the history behind the name is obscure, what is known is that onions abound in this gravy dish. With chicken pieces cooked to perfection with plenty of sliced onion, tomatoes and chillies, it is a dish that goes well with both bread and rice.

Murgh tandoori

For many people tandoori chicken, as this dish is more commonly known the world over, is the king of all Mughlai dishes. Best taken with bread, it is traditionally made in a tandoor where heat from the charcoal gives the chicken its distinctive taste.

Murgh, or chicken, is cleaned and then marinated with a paste comprising not less than 24 powdered spices and condiments. It is either placed whole in the tandoor, or if cut into quarters, placed on skewers and then lowered into the oven. This dish can be prepared on a gas flame but true connoisseurs would argue against it. Nevertheless, home-cooked tandoori chicken on a gas stove has caught on because of the convenience.

Murgh musallam

Here, cubed pieces of chicken are marinated in a fine paste of ginger, garlic, lemon juice and red pepper for at least two hours. It is then cooked on high heat with ghee and beaten yoghurt. The heat is then lowered and the chicken is turned repeatedly until it browns. The dish, which is usually eaten with bread, is garnished with ground almonds, crushed cardamoms and green chillies.

Seek kebab

Kebabs are pieces of mutton grilled over a charcoal fire. *Seek kebab* is easily available and very popular in Muslim-run restaurants and eateries in Delhi. The meat is minced, mixed with onions and spices, shaped and then cooked in a tandoor with metal skewers. Well-cooked *seek kebab* should be crisp on the outside and soft on the inside, and tastes best when eaten hot with chutney, raita or mint sauce. *Seek kebab* is also taken as a snack item. If you are in Old Delhi, enjoy a plate of *seek kebab* with a cup of steaming tea.

Shammi kebab

This is not a kebab dish in the true sense but is actually minced mutton shaped into cutlets. The mince is flavoured with spices, onion, lemon juice, raisins and almonds, and then fried in oil or ghee. Sometimes, an egg would be beaten and added to the meat. These mutton cutlets can be taken as a snack as well as an accompaniment to curry dishes and bread.

Shahi gosht

Also known as 'royal mutton curry' (after the Mughal emperor Shah Jahan), this is lean mutton pieces marinated in spices and salt and added to a mixture of well-fried onions, ginger and garlic paste, green chillies, cumin, mustard and poppy seeds. Water and yoghurt is then added and the meat is cooked on low heat until tender. It is eaten hot with bread or rice. *Gosht*, like *josh* (see *rogan josh* overleaf), is another Hindi word for 'meat'.

Rogan josh

Roghan josh (Kashmiri mutton curry) is an oily dish because quite a lot of vegetable oil or ghee is used. Despite this, the aroma (from cloves, garlic, ginger, pepper, onions, cinnamon, coriander, nutmeg, garam masala and yoghurt) is so lovely that any feeling of queasiness is quickly overtaken by hunger. Tender thigh pieces are gently simmered together with the ingredients over a charcoal fire or a gas stove. If you feel this dish is too oily for your liking, you might want to first skim off the top layer of oil before you help yourself to the meat.

Mutton saag

Here, boneless pieces of mutton are cooked with chopped up spinach leaves (*saag*) in a spicy base of yoghurt, onions, cinnamon, cardamom, coriander and saffron. Although *mutton saag* is very delicious, for some reason it is not one that is prepared in all Delhi eateries. Perhaps spinach alone does not seem to make a great accompaniment with mutton.

Keema matar

This is a must for all lovers of minced meat! Here, mutton is first minced and then cooked in a pressure cooker with *matar*, or green peas. Again, all the major spices — cloves, garlic, ginger, pepper, green chilies, turmeric, cinnamon, cardamom, garam masala, saffron and coriander — are used. Yoghurt, almonds, cashews and nutmeg give this dish its distinctive flavour.

Fish tikka

Here, filleted fish is cut into bite-sized pieces and marinated in a mixture of spices. The most common variety of fish used here is the Singhara (*Mystis Senegala*). The fish pieces are then skewered and grilled over a charcoal fire. This dish is not easily available in Delhi, but where it is offered, it is usually eaten with rice and some gravy-based side dishes.

Tandoor machchi

This dish hails from Peshawar, now in Pakistan and close to the Afghan border. The preferred variety of fish is the Singhara Fish. A whole fish is marinated in a fine paste of coriander leaves, vinegar, red pepper, garlic, ginger, cumin seeds, dried mango leaves, salt, lemon juice and ghee. A skewer is run lengthwise through the body of the fish and then placed in a tandoor. The fish can be prepared equally well over a charcoal grill. It is served with onion rings, chutney and mint sauce and goes with bread.

AN 'EGGETARIAN' IN DELHI?

Within the ambit of non-vegetarian north Indian food would be the use of eggs. Many vegetarians in India would not touch eggs, but there are equally many who love eggs. In Delhi, these people are often called 'eggetarians'! Indeed, in this city, most vegetarian eateries would not serve egg dishes of any sort.

Accompaniments

Indian cuisine is incomplete without accompaniments. In north India, these would be raita and pickles. Chutneys are available, but they are not as popular as pickles and are only taken with certain north Indian dishes

Raita is a yoghurt dish that is seasoned with pepper, salt, lemon juice and flavoured with crushed cumin, cloves or cardamom. Fruit and vegetables are often added to the yoghurt to give a fruit or vegetable raita. Raita, which is almost always served chilled, helps with the digestion of food — especially oily food — and also helps cool the effect of hot curries.

Because of their strong flavour, pickles are taken in small quantities, just enough to add extra taste to the meal. Although pickles are traditionally made at home using recipes passed down from mother to daughter, these days pickles can be bought from grocery stores. Do note that a pickle, for instance mango pickle, in Delhi would taste quite different from one made in Mumbai.

Mixed vegetable raita

This raita dish can be made from any combination of finely shredded vegetables such as carrot, tomatoes, onion and cucumber, with chopped coriander leaves as a garnish. Pepper, cloves and cardamoms are added for extra flavour.

Pineapple raita/fruit raita

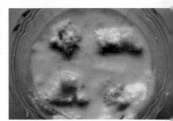

In pineapple raita, chopped pieces of pineapple together with pomegranate and grapes are mixed in a sweetened yoghurt base. Fruit raita, which is not that common, would contain a mix of guava, apple, grapes, mango and melons, depending on their availability.

Aloo mint raita

The main ingredient in this dish is *aloo*, or potato, which has been boiled and diced. Small pieces of mint leaves are added to give a refreshing taste.

Boondi raita

This popular raita has its roots in the desert state of Rajasthan. *Boondis* are tiny fried golden yellow balls made of gram flour or split-pea flour mixed with sugar and salt. In Hindi, *boond* means a 'drop'. The *boondis* are cooled and added to yoghurt seasoned with pepper and fresh mint or coriander. The raita is kept in the refrigerator until ready to be served.

Pudina raita

This cool and refreshing raita is made with a paste of mint (*pudina*) and chillies mixed with yoghurt and salt. Some people add pomegranate and pepper.

Pickles

In north India, pickles are usually made of vegetables or fruit in a special mix of mustard oil, spices (*ajwain* and fennel) and salt, with vinegar as a souring agent. Although mango, lime and Indian gooseberry (a fruit rich in Vitamin C and indigenous to India) are traditionally used to make pickles, the range has expanded to include almost every other fruit and vegetable, such as carrot, radish, green and red chillies, aubergine, bitter gourd, ginger, cauliflower, drumstick, onion, tomato, garlic and green peas. Pickles complement both rice and north Indian bread meals. On the streets, pickles are even served with paratha.

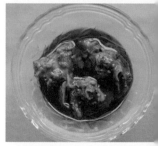

Vegetable salad

Salads are popular in Delhi and are eaten for their digestive benefits. The ingredients in this salad dish include sliced carrot, radish (and its leaves), cauliflower leaves, onion, tomatoes, lettuce, beetroot and coriander leaves. The salad is seasoned with some lemon juice and ground pepper.

Chutney

The most common north Indian chutneys are made from mint leaves, mangoes and tomatoes. Mint chutney is the most popular and is usually served with snacks such as samosas and *aloo tikki*. Mint chutney is a blend of fresh mint and coriander leaves, green chillies, sliced onions, lemon juice, water and salt. Some people would also add tamarind, mustard seeds, a pinch of sugar and asafoetida. It can be made thick although vendors usually serve the watery version. The other popular north Indian chutneys are mango chutney and tomato chutney.

Most restaurants in Delhi do not offer raita free and you will have to order it separately. The same goes for salads. However, pickles and onions (the latter often dipped in vinegar) usually come gratis with a main meal. Although chutneys are available, they are not always provided in restaurants. Where chutney is served with snacks, it would be given without charge.

Desserts

Indian desserts range from the mildly sweet to those dripping with sugar, so weight watchers… beware! Although drinking coffee or tea after dinner is popular among the more sophisticated Indians, these beverages cannot compete with desserts when it comes to winding up an Indian meal.

Indian desserts can be broadly divided into two categories: those with milk and those without. Some Indian desserts are taken during the main course. This is especially true of kheer and the various kinds of *halwa*, but as it often happens in India, what could be part of the main dish for some is a dessert for others.

Wherever in Delhi you are having a traditional north Indian meal, desserts will always be on the menu. If overly sweet desserts are not your cup of tea, ask the waiter for one that is not too sweet. Do note that there is no fixed formula when it comes to 'sweetness' ratings — a bowl of carrot fudge made by one eatery might be less sweet compared to that offered at another.

Kulfi

Kulfi is India's answer to ice cream and remains a firm favourite despite the immense popularity of ice cream in the country. Made with milk, almonds and pistachios, kulfi is quite a rich dessert. It is prepared in conical shaped tins or aluminium moulds and left to freeze in crushed

ice. It is usually served with a helping of *phaluda* (this is made of corn flour and looks like macaroni). Occasionally, sweet syrup might be poured over the *phaluda*. If you do not have a sweet tooth, ask for *kulfi* without the *phaluda* and syrup.

Gulab jamun

This is a dessert that first-timers might find too sweet and overpowering. Resembling preserved plums, it can be described as the Indian equivalent to cream cheese and is very popular all over the country. *Gulab jamun* is a dessert of deep-fried milk balls

soaked in thick sugar syrup. The dough for the milk balls is made from a soft cream cheese called *chhena* and dried whole milk known as *khoya*. When the dough is of the right consistency, it is rolled into balls, fried until golden brown and then kept aside until served. Only then are the balls put into the syrup where they turn spongy. *Gulab jamun* is best eaten while hot.

Kheer

Kheer is a rice pudding which can be eaten hot or cold. The rice is first soaked for about 30 minutes and then cooked. A pot of milk is put to the boil to which sugar is added. When the milk is boiling, the rice is poured into the pot and stirred until

the mixture becomes creamy. It is then left to cool. When ready to be served, it is topped with powdered cardamom seeds, finely sliced pistachios and almonds.

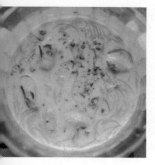

Sevaien kheer

Sevaien kheer, or vermicelli milk pudding, is associated with Eid-ul-Fitr, an important religious festival celebrated by Indian Muslims. It is a concoction of fresh boiled milk (either cow or buffalo milk), ghee, sugar, wheat flour vermicelli, saffron, cardamom, clove, almonds and pistachios. The dessert is mostly prepared thick but can be watery, too.

Sabudana kheer

In this dessert *sabudana*, or sago beans, are added to boiling milk and served. As sago beans are an important source of energy, it is an appropriate dish for people, especially the elderly, who find it difficult to digest 'heavy' foods.

Gajar halwa

Halwa is the Arabic word for 'fudge' and *gajar halwa* (or carrot fudge) is a popular sweet dish of Mughal origin. Besides carrot, which forms the base, the ingredients that go into making the fudge include sugar, ghee, cardamoms, almonds, pistachios, granulated *khoya* and silver foil. For the best carrot fudge in Delhi, go to Old Delhi's Ballimaran Street.

Suji halwa

This popular fudge dessert can be mildly sweet or extremely sweet. Its dominant ingredient is semolina that is stirred on slow fire with ghee and a mixture of sugar, saffron, pistachios, almonds, cardamom and water. It is normally served hot but can be eaten cold, too.

Shrikhand (creamy yoghurt)

In this dessert, fresh yoghurt is whipped up and mixed with *jaggery* (unrefined sugar from the juice of crushed sugar cane) and dried fruit. Shrikhand is also the name of the refined jaggery powder that tastes good even if eaten raw. Shrikhand is served both cold or at room temperature.

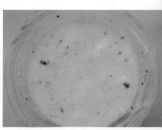

Indian fruit salad

Highly popular in restaurants and at marriage ceremonies, this is the usual ice cream mixed with pieces of pineapple, mango, melon, grapes, guava, banana and papaya. It is a fitting dessert to conclude a meal.

Saunf

In addition to paan, you will notice the locals chewing on a spice at the end of a meal. This spice is aniseed, or *saunf*. Is it a mouth freshener or a digestive aid? Well, it does both jobs very well. Believed to 'cure' flatulence and help with digestion at the end of a meal for its digestive properties, it comes gratis in restaurants. The spice, which looks very much like white cumin seeds, is offered either plain or mixed with sugar. You will sometimes see multi-coloured *saunf*; these have been coated with artificial colouring.

Street food

When it comes to street food, no Indian city offers more variety than Delhi. For less than US$1, it is easy to fill up on snacks such as golgappa, *papdi chaat*, *chole kulche*, *chole bhature*, fruit chaat, fresh fruit or sugarcane juice, *aloo tikki* or bread *pakoda*. There is also a thriving market for burgers stuffed with mashed potato and onion, as well as boiled eggs and fluffy omelettes, all of which come with tomato sauce. Even south Indian snacks like dosa, vada and idli can be easily found on Delhi streets.

Golgappa

Try this if you like something tangy. Known as *pani-puri* in Mumbai, golgappas are small hollow puffs made of wheat flour and semolina. The vendor makes a small hole in each piece, filling it with a mixture of mashed chickpeas and potatoes and some sweet chutney. It is then dipped into a watery brew containg cumin seeds and tamarind.

Papdi

Vendors selling golgappa will also offer *papdi*. These are crisp discs of refined flour (about 2.5 cm in diameter) fried in ghee and served with mashed potatoes, mango chutney and yoghurt. These are also served cold. When you finish a plate of *papdi*, vendors will be happy to serve you, for free, the same tangy cumin seed/tamarind water that they give with golgappa.

Aloo tikki

I know of expatriates who simply cannot do without these potato cakes! Made from mashed boiled potatoes and lentils, and seasoned with black pepper powder, black salt, chopped green chillies and coriander leaves, they make a hearty and filling snack. The vendor takes a handful of the mixture and shapes them into small cakes, or *tikki*. These are shallow-fried in vegetable oil and served with mango and/or mint chutney.

Bhelpuri

This snack comes from Mumbai and is very popular in Delhi. It is a mixture of thin deep-fried chickpea flour noodles, flaked rice known as *murmure*, chopped onion, chopped green chillies, coriander, roasted cumin seeds, black pepper, tamarind and *jaggery* that is seasoned with lemon juice. It has a pungent yet sweet taste.

CHAAT

The word chaat comes from the Hindi word *chaatna*, which means 'licking'. It is a generic term for any tangy snack item. For instance, a plate of *papdi* may also be known as *papdi* chaat while *aloo tikki*, bhelpuri and golgappa are also seen as chaat items. Even cut fruit sold on the street with a sprinkling of lemon juice and black pepper qualifies as fruit chaat. What is common among all chaat items is the use of spices. A chaat *wala* on the streets of Delhi would be one selling golgappa, *aloo tikki* and papdi.

Pakoda

These are savoury fritters made from vegetables mixed in a paste of gram flour and deep-fried in vegetable oil. The vegetables are often chopped spinach leaves (for which you get *palak pakoda*), cauliflower florets (*gobi pakoda*) or whole green chillies (*green chilli pakoda*). Except for the green chilli fritters, the other two take no particular shape and you will sometimes see bits of spinach or cauliflower sticking out. These snacks come with tomato sauce. The green chilli fritters can be very hot.

Another type of pakoda is *bread pakoda*. Here, bread is sliced into two and filled with paneer or mashed potatoes. The bread is then dipped into a batter of *besan* and fried in oil. When ready, garam masala is sprinkled to give added taste.

Jalebi

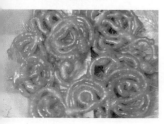

This is another popular sweet snack, and for the best jalebi go to Old Delhi. It can be very sweet and is served hot. The batter for jalebi is made of gram flour, refined flour, yoghurt, sugar and saffron. This is transferred to a piping bag (often made of muslin cloth). The batter is squeezed out in whirls into a pan of hot ghee where they are deep fried until they turn golden yellow

Samosa

From Sydney to New York, people love samosas for their taste. Samosas are flour-based pastries stuffed with a savoury filling, usually coarsely mashed potatoes and peas flavoured with spices. Meat can be used, but this is rare in Delhi. Samosas are deep-fried and taste best when eaten piping hot.

North Indian restaurants

Al Kakori

🪑 30 Vasant Place Market, R K Puram

🚗 9km

🕐 6:30pm–11:00pm

💲💲   🖩 Cash only

𝒶𝒷𝒸   📞 2610-4101

A friendly place with efficient service, Al Kakori draws customers with its mouth watering kebabs, which are also served wrapped in *rumali roti*. Although not on the tourist circuit, it makes kebabs that are worth venturing out for.

Amber

🪑 N19 Connaught Circus

🚗 Walking distance

🕐 11:00am–11:00pm

💲💲💲💲 🖩 Cash and credit card

𝒶𝒷𝒸   📞 2331-2092 / 2373-6485

Located in the very heart of Delhi, Amber tends to get very crowded during lunch hours. It serves up a variety of roti and paratha, and its best selling dish is chicken *seek kebab*. Delhites rave about the freshness of its Russian salad and green salad. Dial-A-Meal service is available here.

Anand Restaurant

🪑 Off Janpath, Connaught Place

🚗 Walking distance; behind Scindia House

🕐 9:00am–11:00pm

💲💲   🖩 Cash only

𝒶𝒷𝒸   📞 2331-3349

This place serves good Punjabi fare including breakfast. Among the best items on the menu are *dal makhni*, *shahi paneer*, butter chicken, tandoori chicken and chicken biryani. Round off your meal with gulab jamun, a sweet dessert that you can buy from one of two small shops near the restaurant.

Angeethi

 Asian Games Village Restaurant Complex, Siri Fort Marg

 10km

🕐 7:30pm–11:30pm

💲 💲 💲   Cash and credit card

       ☎ 2649-2348 / 2649-3628

This place is well known for its open kitchen where one can see the cooks at work. Its signature dish is mutton masala *tak-a-tak*. Equally worth trying are tandoori fish and butter chicken. There is a paan kiosk just outside. Why not try a *meeta* paan after a satisfying dinner?

Baujee da Dhaba

 18 Hauz Khas Village, Hauz Khas

 10km

🕐 Noon–4:00pm, 7:00pm–Midnight

💲 💲   Cash and credit card

       ☎ 2652-5511 / 2652-7910

The interior has a rustic decor; its walls are plastered with mud and adorned with folk paintings. Curries, biryanis and kebabs are served in copper pots. Try its *murgh makhni*, dal and *jeera matar*. Dial-A-Meal service is available here.

Bengali Sweet House

 27–37 Bengali Market, Babar Road

 3km

🕐 8:00am–11:00pm

💲   Cash and credit card

      ☎ 2331-9224 / 2331-1855

With a reputation for great tasting snacks, Bengali Sweets (as it is popularly known) is a hit with office workers, students and shoppers in nearby Connaught Place. Best selling items are golgappa, samosa and kulfi. Loyal customers say this is the best place to get *dahi vada* and *aloo tikki*.

Bukhara

Maurya Sheraton and Towers, Sadar Patel Marg

6km

Noon–3:00pm, 7:00pm–11:30pm

Cash and credit card

2611-2233

If not for its pricey meals, Bukhara could well stand up to the illustrious Karim in Old Delhi any day. Among the city's luxury hotels, connoisseurs say this is the best place to savour Mughlai cuisine. In the hands of highly skilled chefs, it serves excellent roti, kebabs, chicken tikka, butter chicken and *dal makhni*. Bukhara's reputation was recently boosted with the visit of the former US president Bill Clinton and his daughter Chelsea. Today, it offers two thali-like meals — a non-vegetarian Presidential Platter and a vegetarian Chelsea Platter.

Café Masala

A12 Connaught Place

Walking distance

Noon–Midnight

Cash and credit card

5528-5749

This is Delhi's first weigh-and-pay restaurant. You get to choose what you want and the quantity from a selection of dishes spread out buffet-style. Except for roti, which is charged by the piece, rice and side dishes are sold by weight. Vegetarian dishes cost Rs.18 per 100 grams, while meat dishes cost Rs.30 per 100 grams. With the menu overseen by Master Chef Sitangsu Chakravarty (see pages 161–162 for more information about the chef), you can be sure of getting your money's worth.

Chic Fish

32 Corner Market, Malviya Nagar

12km

6:00pm–11:00pm. Closed on Tuesdays

Cash only

2668-0404

The location may not be great, being situated off a traffic-choked street in south Delhi, but it enjoys a regular customer base. Highly recommended are tandoori chicken, butter chicken and the delicately-cooked fish tikka.

Chor Bizarre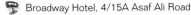

Broadway Hotel, 4/15A Asaf Ali Road

6km

Noon–Midnight

$ $ $ Cash and credit card

      2327-3821

With a name that translates to 'Thieves Market', Chor Bizarre is popular for its authentic Kashmiri food, especially its melt-in-the-mouth mutton *yakhni* and mutton *gushtaba*. The restaurant is decorated with old records and movie posters, gramophones and other antiques. Old style leg-driven sewing machines have been converted to dining tables. Even the salad spread is displayed in a vintage car! All in, this place is worth every rupee spent.

Colonel's Kababz

Defence Colony Flyover Market, Defence Colony

7km

11:00am–Midnight

$ $ Cash and credit card

       2433-3121 / 2433-0136

Colonel's Kababz offers both dine-in as well as takeaway services. Its most popular dishes are chicken *seek*, mutton *seek*, butter chicken, *malai kofta* and *jeera aloo*. Dial-A-Meal service is available here.

Copper Chimney

Bhanot Corner, Pamposh Enclave, Greater Kailash 1

10km

Noon–3:15pm, 7:30pm–Midnight

$ $ $ Cash and credit card

       2641-3999 / 2848-2456

Loyal customers say this restaurant serves authentic Punjabi food and they go there to feast on its chicken dishes in particular *murgh kadhai* and chicken *bagani bahar*. Also popular are *matar paneer* and naan, especially butter naan, keema naan and *kabuli* naan. Dial-A-Meal service is available here.

Corbett's

🍴 The Claridges Hotel, Aurangazeb Road

🧭 4km

🕐 Noon–3:00pm, 7:30pm–11:30pm

💲💲💲💲　　　　　　　　💳 Cash and credit card

🔤　　　　　　　　　　　📞 2301-0211

Named after the celebrated hunter Jim Corbett, the decor in this restaurant is enough to make a special visit. The interior replicates the wild and even boasts an artificial stream! Corbett's is located in one of Delhi's oldest exclusive hotels. Serves excellent tandoori dishes, chicken tikka, tandoori prawn and chicken *tak-a-tak*. Weekends are always crowded.

Deez Biryani Corner

🍴 Defence Colony Flyover Market, Defence Colony

🧭 7km

🕐 11:00am–11:00pm

💲💲　　　　　　　　　💳 Cash and credit card

🔤 🏠　　　　　　　　　📞 2469-0067 / 5155-1515

Delhites come to this small eatery when they want to bring home delicious mutton, chicken or fish biryani. Whether it is for a cosy family dinner for two or for a party of 60, Deez Biryani Corner provides reliable takeaway services and food that does not disappoint. There are dine-in facilities as well.

Dhaba

🍴 The Claridges Hotel, Aurangazeb Road

🧭 4km

🕐 12:30pm–2:30pm, 8:00pm–11:30pm

💲💲💲💲　　　　　　　　💳 Cash and credit card

🔤　　　　　　　　　　　📞 2301-0211

Dhaba is the Hindi word for the typical roadside eateries that dot the Indian highways; these eateries sprouted up to feed hungry truck drivers. True to its name, a model of a truck greets visitors to Dhaba. The restaurant has earned a reputation for delicious north Indian vegetarian and non-vegetarian fare. Try the butter chicken, curry chicken, chicken tikka, stuffed aubergine and dal.

Dhaha — A Punjabi Theme

 A5 Vishal Enclave, Rajouri Garden

 10km

 Noon–11:30pm

      Cash only

     2542-0303 / 2546-0101

Popular with families, this restaurant is located in a predominantly Punjabi neighbourhood away from the tourist circuit. It serves the residents well with authentic Punjabi food. Try its butter chicken.

Dilli Haat

 Aurobindo Marg

 7km; opposite INA Market

 11:00am–9:30pm

 Cash only

     2611-9UJ / 2467-8817

Dilli Haat is one of two good food courts in Delhi and the more popular one, too. Located in a shopping complex of the same name where handicrafts are sold, it is the place to sample all the various regional cuisines that India has to offer under one roof.

The quality of food is good in most stalls. For north Indian and other cuisine, try the following: meat balls and *paneer chaman* from Jammu and Kashmir; prawn cutlets and *kobiraji* chicken from West Bengal; chicken curry from Assam; and from Rajasthan, the thali which comes with vegetables and two types of roti. From Maharashtra try *zunka bhakir*, roti made from mixed cereals and served with aubergine; *thali peeth*, roti made from 14 types of cereal; and *pav bhaji*, roti served with spicy mashed tomatoes and potatoes.

If you crave for chaat items and *chole bhatura*, head for Delhi Restaurant in Dilli Haat. There is also a stall that serves only Indian coffee, and good coffee at that.

Note that there is a nominal entry fee of Rs.10 (Rs.5 for children) to enter the shopping centre which, incidentally, is also one of few public places in the city that is disabled-friendly.

Dum Pukht

Hotel Maurya Sheraton, Sardar Patel Marg

5km

7:30pm–11:30pm. Open on Sundays for lunch

$ $ $ $ $ $ Cash and credit card

abc   2611-2233

Although very expensive, Dum Pukht is rated very highly and said to carry on a 200-year-old cuisine from the northern region of Awadh (present-day Uttar Pradesh). Popular items on its menu are tikkas, kebabs, roti, naan, dal and stuffed aubergine. This is a place to go for excellent food.

Eatopia

India Habitat Centre, Lodi Road

4km

Noon–11:00pm

$ Cash only

abc   2468-2222

Like Dilli Haat, this is a self-service food court where you pay first and then eat. Although it can hold only about 200 people, it is popular especially during weekends and holidays.There are not very many stalls, but you will be able to sample north Indian, Chinese and Thai food. There is a stall selling roti and dishes as well as a chaat corner. Prices are very reasonable.

Embassy Restaurant

11D Connaught Place

Walking distance

10:00am–11.30pm

$ $ $ Cash and credit card

abc   2341-6434 / 2341-7480

This restaurant is an institution in Delhi and very popular with the city's politicians, journalists and retired bureaucrats. Being centrally located, it also attracts shoppers, office workers and tourists who go there for its north Indian cuisine, snacks and coffee. Some items to try are chicken and egg pakoda, mushroom on toast and club sandwich, which is a combination of mutton, chicken and cheese.

Essex Farm

 Aurobindo Marg

 12km; junction of Aurobindo Marg and IIT

 12:30pm–3:00pm, 7:30pm–11:00pm

  Cash and credit card

  2652-4040 / 2696-3537

The land on which this restaurant occupies was once a poultry farm. Essex Farm is popular for its vegetarian and non-vegetarian north Indian dishes. Highly rated are its tandoori dishes. There is a bowling alley just outside the dining section.

Gulati Restaurant

 Pandara Road Market, Pandara Road

 6km

 Noon–1:30am

 Cash and credit card

  2338-8836

Another immensely popular restaurant, Gulati's clientele includes Bollywood movie stars. Not only does it offer value for money, many Delhites swear it is one of the city's best restaurants. If the crowds that throng it until late into the night are any indication, it may well be the best. *Dal makhni*, *shahi paneer*, chicken tikka and butter naan are always in demand. Dial-A-Meal service is available here.

HariChatni.com

 PVR Cinema Complex, Saket

 14km

 11:00am–11:00pm

  Cash only

  98109-64884

This simple, open air restaurant is located close to the well-known PVR movie theatre. Try its *palak paneer*, *gobi masala*, butter chicken and *rumali roti*. When dinner is over, buy a *meeta* paan from the paan *wala* who is always stationed nearby. The area also hosts a number of other restaurants serving a wide variety of cuisine.

Have More

 Pandara Road Market, Pandara Road

 6km; near the India Gate

 Noon–11:30pm

  Cash and credit card

  ☎ 2338-7070 / 2338-7171

Have More is one of the more popular restaurants that you can find in the area. Serving excellent Punjabi food, regulars attest to its chicken *do-pyaza*, *shahi paneer*, *dal makhni* and *dal tadka*.

Kake Da Hotel

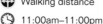 Municipal Market, Outer Circle, Connaught Circus

 Walking distance

 11:00am–11:00pm

 Cash and credit card

  ☎ 2341-1580

An unpretentious Punjabi restaurant, Kake Da Hotel appeared on the scene soon after India's independence in 1947 when Punjabis made Delhi their home (many had fled the newly-created Muslim majority Pakistan). But it is a crammed place and if you are looking to have a relaxed meal, this cannot be your choice. It boasts leading politicians among its customers. The market where this eatery is located is more popularly known as Shankar Market.

Karim

 Gali Kababiyan

 10km; near Jama Masjid

 Noon–3:30pm, 6:30pm–11:30pm. Closed on Tuesdays

 Cash and credit card

☎ 2326-9880 / 2326-4981

Karim serves delicious Mughlai food, and is a must for anyone who loves chicken and mutton. Every dish on the menu is worth trying but I would recommend the chicken curry, *murgh musallam* and chicken tikka. Take a stroll after your meal around the congested but lively area that surrounds the restaurant. Nearby is Jama Masjid and not far away is the imposing Red Fort. Note that Karim and its three other outlets do not serve lunch during the Muslim fasting month of Ramadan. Dial-A-Meal service is available. (See pages 164–166 for more about Karim.)

Kashmiri Food Centre

 C6/6036 Vasant Kunj

16km

No fixed operating hours

💲 💲 💲   Cash only

ab   ☎ 2689-5871

Despite its name, this is not a food centre in the real sense of the word. The owners operate a takeaway service from a home. You place the order and pick up the food. They make delicious Kashmiri food, both vegetarian and non-vegetarian, and the quality is as good as that of Chor Bizarre. Among its outstanding items are *rogan josh, yakhni, khatti dal* and *khatti bhindi* (Lady's Fingers).

Kwality

Regal Building, Connaught Place

Walking distance

Noon–11:00pm

💲 💲 💲   Cash and credit card

ab   ☎ 2374-2310 / 2374-2352

This 1940s restaurant is still going strong by virtue of the quality food it serves. Always in demand are *chole bhatura*, which is rated among the best in the city, as well as its chicken, fish and mutton tikka. Originally an ice cream parlour, the desserts they offer include gulab jamun and Kwality special pudding. Dial-A-Meal service is available here.

Madhuban Restaurant

PVR Cinema Complex, Saket

15km

Noon–11:00pm

💲 💲   Cash and credit card

ab 🏠   ☎ 2696-5047 / 2651-8687

Although less well known than other restaurants, this is a good place for north Indian food. If you are watching a movie at PVR Saket, do walk over for a meal and try their *nav rattan korma*, butter chicken, *palak paneer* and dal. End the night with a paan from the paan *wala* opposite the restaurant and a browse through the many new and second-hand bookstores in the vicinity.

Mini Mughal

1/6 Jor Bagh Market, Lodi Road

5km

12:30pm–3:30pm, 7:00pm–11:30pm

Cash and credit card

2461-7979 / 2464-6900

A small but highly respected restaurant that offers value for money. It is located in a residential area where many expatriates live and they make up its regular clients. Highly recommended dishes are mutton kebab, butter chicken, *dal tadka* and green chilli naan. Dial-A-Meal service is available here.

Moti Mahal

3704 Netaji Subhash Marg, Daryaganj

4km; near Golcha Cinema

11:00am–Midnight

Cash and credit card

2327-3011 / 2327-3661

This is another of Delhi's legendary restaurants that came up in the aftermath of India's independence. Located in the very busy Daryaganj area, it is not as popular as it used to be, but its Punjabi and Mughlai fare still draws a good crowd.

Moti Mahal Deluxe

Defence Colony Market, Defence Colony

7km

Noon–11:30pm

Cash and credit card

2433-0263 / 2433-0265

Located in an upper class south Delhi neighbourhood, Moti Mahal Deluxe is a favourite choice for those seeking out butter chicken, *dal makhni* and tikka dishes. The naan it serves is among the best in the city. Dial-A-Meal service is available here.

Nathu's Sweets

🍴 Bengali Market

🧭 3km

🕐 9:00am–11:00pm

💲

📠 Cash and credit card

2372-0099 / 2372-0088

Providing direct competition to Bengali Sweet House is its neighbour, Nathu's Sweets. For less than Rs.100, you can have your fill of *chaat papdi*, golgappa, *chole bhatura* and kulfi. And if you want Indian sweets, this is the place.

Nirula's

🍴 L Block, Connaught Place

🧭 Walking distance

🕐 10:00am–11:00pm

💲💲

📠 Cash and credit card

2341-7419

This is Delhi's original fast food chain, and this is where many Delhites — now in their 40s and older — would go for a burger or sandwich. Today, global fast food restaurants have crept into India in a big way, but Nirula's has managed to retain its charms even with some 20 branches under its belt. It is a one-stop centre for north and south Indian food as well as western-style breakfast (omelettes, cinammon rolls and Danish pastries), burgers and pizzas. North Indian items on its menu include *paneer pakoda* and tandoori chicken.

Nizam's Kathi Kabab

🍴 Plaza Building, Connaught Place

🧭 Walking distance

🕐 11:00am–11:00pm

💲💲

📠 Cash only

2371-3078 / 5151-346

A popular hangout for office workers and shoppers in the area, Nizam is known for its wide variety of rolls filled with cottage cheese, potato or mushroom, but the ones always in demand are its double chick roll and double egg roll. If you want a quick meal, then Nizam's Ka Kabab is for you.

Pandit Gaya Prasad Shiv Charan Parathe Wale

1974 Gali Parathe Wali, Chandni Chowk

11km

9:00am–11:00pm

Cash only

2327-6612

This is one among several shops that line a narrow lane off Chandni Chowk, appropriately called Parathe Wali Gali (Paratha Lane). The owners say that the shops came up during Mughal rule and that they have been selling paratha ever since. This outlet serves several types of paratha including *aloo paratha*, *mooli paratha*, dal paratha, paneer paratha, *pudina paratha*, *gobi paratha* and mixed paratha — all these come with free helpings of mango chutney, pickles and two vegetables. Do not drink the water there but try the lassi.

Park Balluchi

Inside Deer Park, Hauz Khas

10km

Noon–Midnight

Cash and credit card

2685-9369

The location is great — on the edge of a park where there is a mini zoo filled with deer, peacocks and rabbits. Park Balluchi has a good range of vegetarian and non-vegetarian food including tandoori, dal and paneer dishes. Naan and roti are said to be good. But go only if you have a car to bring you back; finding an auto might pose a problem especially at night. Dial-A-Meal service is available here.

Pindi

Pandara Road Market, Pandara Road

6km

Noon–Midnight

Cash and credit card

2338-8703 / 2338-7832

This restaurant offers excellent vegetarian and non-vegetarian fare. Its butter chicken and chicken tikka are very popular. Expect crowds during weekends and holidays.

Pragati Maidan Complex

 Mathura Road

 3km

🕐 11:00am–11:00pm

 $ $ Cash and credit card

 _ab_   ☎ 2237-1111

This is not a restaurant but a group of eateries located in a trade fair complex close to Delhi Zoo and the Old Fort. Unlike Dilli Haat, the stalls are not situated next to each other. Stalls worth trying for north Indian food are Balluchi Tandoor Junction, Bharatiyam, Family's Delight and Rave Café, which also serves Spanish Omelette and ice cream.

Punjabi By Nature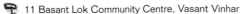

 11 Basant Lok Community Centre, Vasant Vinhar

 12km

🕐 12:30pm–3:00pm, 7:30pm–11:00pm

 $ $ $ Cash and credit card

 _ab_   ☎ 5151-6666 / 5151-6667

You get excellent Punjabi food and friendly service here. The music may be loud but if you can put up with that, you will get to taste delicious _shahi paneer_ and butter chicken. One of its specialities is golgappa, which they serve with vodka instead of the usual tamarind and cumin seed water. Dial-A-meal service is available here.

Rajinder da Dhaba

 AB 14 Safdarjung Enclave

 10km; near the (former) Kamal Cinema

 5:00pm–11:00pm

 $ $ Cash only

 _ab_   ☎ 98111-06326

This is not a restaurant but a roadside eatery, truly a _dhaba_. You pay for the food, collect it and then locate a table. There are no chairs, so you stand and eat. A piece of tandoori roti or _rumali roti_ costs as little as Rs.3... no wonder it is always crowded. Items worth trying are fish tikka, _seek kebab_, butter chicken and roast chicken.

Standard Restaurant

Regal Building, Connaught Place

Walking distance; above Regal Theatre

11:00am–Midnight

Cash and credit card

2336-0048 / 2374-4688

Established in the 1950s, Standard Restaurant specialises in both north Indian and south Indian cuisine. One reason for its continuing success has been attributed to its location above the landmark Regal Theatre, where you get a panoramic view of the perenially busy Connaught Place. Good north Indian dishes to try are fish tikka and tandoori chicken. Try its Espresso Coffee, which always comes with special chocolate biscuits.

Sweets Corner

Sundar Nagar Market, Sundar Nagar

5km

7:00am–11:00pm

Cash and credit card

5150-7000 / 5151-7002

Located in a quiet part of Delhi close to the imposing Old Fort, Sweets Corner is known for its mainly north Indian snacks. Make a detour here to try its *aloo tikki*, golgappa, puri, *chole bhatura*, vada and dosa.

Tee Pee O

118–119 Mohan Singh Place, Connaught Place

Walking distance; near Rivoli Cinema

11:00am–11:00pm

Cash only

2336-1550

This small and old restaurant, located in a corner of a shopping centre, still draws the crowds who come for its simple yet tasty chicken and mutton biryani. You will be disappointed if you want ambience as it has none, but the food makes up for it. Backpackers are a common sight here and they come for hot tea infused with ginger and cardamom. It is estimated that the eatery sells up to 2000 cups of tea a day!

Temptation

Shanti Niketan Market, Shanti Niketan

8km

11:00am–10:00pm

Cash only

2410-6812 / 2410-6814

There is one waiter here and he deserves an Olympic Gold for efficiency! Located in an area where many diplomats reside, this eatery has five indoor tables and six outside for al fresco dining. Some of the dishes it offers are rather oily; still, worth trying are dal, *gobi masala* and chicken dishes.

The Great Kebab Factory

Hotel Raddison, National Highway 8, Mahipalpur

20km; close to Indira Gandhi International Airport

7:30pm–11:00pm. Open on Sundays for lunch

Cash and credit card

2677-9191

This expensive restaurant is worth splurging on. It serves excellent vegetarian and non-vegetarian food, buffet style. But here, you do not go to the food... the food comes to you! Once you take your seat, waiter after waiter comes to your table, bearing one delicacy after another. The march past is unending, until you decide you have had enough and ask for the bill. Try the kebabs and chicken dishes. If you are vegetarian, you will enjoy its *paneer tikka*. A treat awaits on Sunday afternoons — beer is complimentary until 3:00pm. To enjoy the same food at perhaps half the price, head for its branch at 31–32 Central Market, Punjabi Bagh (tel: 2522-1171).

The Rampur Kitchen

8A Khan Market

6km

Noon–11:30pm

Cash and credit card

2460-3366

Connoisseurs recommend this restaurant for its stuffed tandoori *aloo*, mutton stew, mutton *murgh rampuri*, *rampuri dal* and vegetable *nav rattan korma*. The mixed vegetable raita is also very good.

Triveni Tea Terrace 🍴

205 Tan Sen Marg, Triveni Kala Sangam

3km; near Mandi House

10:00am–3:00pm, 4:00pm–6:30pm

Cash only

2371-8833

Located near the Bengali Market, this place attracts writers and artists who come mainly for its vegetarian fare. Try the paratha and *jeera aloo*, which are highly recommended. The restaurant can get crowded during lunch hours.

United Coffee House 🍴

E15 Connaught Place

Walking distance

9:30am–Midnight

Cash and credit card

2341-1697

Established in the 1950s and spread over two floors, United Coffee House enjoys the patronage of loyal cutsomers and tourists. It serves a variety of cuisine, but it would be best to stick to north Indian dishes. Try the *chole bhatura* and mutton samosa.

Village Mohalla

12 Hauz Khas Village

8km

11:00am–11:00pm

Cash and credit card

2685-3857 / 2685-2227

Located in an area popular with foreigners, Village Mohalla offers good chicken dishes such as *murgh kali mirch*. Its vegetarian offering, *kadhai paneer*, is highly recommended.

Waves

 A4 Sarvodaya Enclave, Aurobindo Marg

 13km; near Aurobindo Ashram

 11:00am–Midnight

 Cash and credit card

 5168-1333 / 5168-1444

With a pleasing decor and a huge lawn for children to run around, Waves is an ideal place to bring your family. Regular customers highly recommend the various tikka dishes.

York Restaurant

 K10 Connaught Circus

 Walking distance

 11:00am–Midnight

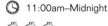

 Cash and credit card

 2341-5769

This is another of Delhi's pre-independence restaurants, located in what was then the city's only commercial district. York Restaurant offers a very good range of both vegetarian and non-vegetarian north Indian fare. Apart from *seek kebab* and tandoori items, it serves good *dal makhni* and *matar paneer*. The naan and paratha are good, too.

South
Indian cuisine

After India achieved independence in 1947 many south Indians started to migrate to Delhi in search of jobs, but it took Delhites many more years before they had their first taste of south Indian food. This was not without reason. The initial waves of south Indians were mostly blue-collar workers who were content to eat at home and did not venture into culinary business. However, once the craze for south Indian cuisine caught on, there was no stopping it. Today, eateries offering south Indian food can be found all over Delhi, with many of them employing Tamil cooks. Although south Indian cuisine boasts many outstanding non-vegetarian dishes, these are not easily available in Delhi. Most south Indian restaurants in the city serve vegetarian food mainly because there is already a wide range of tempting north Indian meat dishes.

Appetisers

If you venture into any south Indian restaurant in Delhi, the appetisers you will get are crispy crackers called pappadam and a tangy soup known as rasam. This is quite unlike north Indian cuisine where fruit juice, lassi and *jal jeera*, or cumin seed water, are taken to start off a meal. Nonetheless, many south Indian restaurants would also serve fruit juice or lassi to cater to the tastes of all their customers.

Pappadam

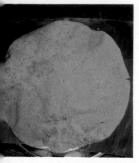

Pappadam are deep-fried crackers made from *urad* dal, or black gram lentil. North Indians call these crackers 'papad'. Delhi food outlets serving south Indian fare almost always offer the plain variety, which does not contain garlic or peppercorns. In these eateries, pappadam would be served as an appetiser together with a bowl of rasam, although people will continue to have the crackers with the rest of the meal.

It is easy to spot south Indians just by observing how they eat pappadam — they tend to break up the crackers into small pieces and mix them into the rice.

Rasam

Rasam is the name given to a light and watery soup that is quintessentially south Indian. Although light, it is immensely satisfying. The main ingredients are tomatoes and tamarind, both of which give the soup a tangy, slightly sour taste. Other basic ingredients include curry leaves, pepper, cumin seeds and mustard seeds. There are many types of rasam depending on what other ingredient is added. Some popular preparations of rasam are tomato rasam, lime rasam and garlic rasam. One preparation, cumin and black pepper rasam, is so hot and spicy it is potent enough to stop a cold in its tracks.

RASAM

In a typical south Indian meal, piping hot rasam is served as a second course (the first course being *sambar*, which is a vegetable dish in a base of lentil gravy). South Indians like to wet their rice with rasam and eat the rice with pappadam and an assortment of side dishes, such as lentils, vegetables and yoghurt. Unless one is having a traditional south Indian rice meal (which is called a thali), in Delhi eateries rasam is most often served as a soup ahead of snack items.

Rice

Rice is the staple of choice in south Indian meals. Not only is rice steamed and eaten with accompanying dishes or cooked with a variety of condiments, rice also constitutes the base for many south Indian snacks such as dosa and idli (see pages 105–107). Where rice is steamed, the long-grained basmati variety is the rice of choice. When it comes to making snacks, two short-grained varieties are used: *parmal* rice and *sela* rice. Some south Indian rice dishes, such as tamarind rice, are so filling they can be eaten as a meal on their own. The rice dishes featured here can only be found in vegetarian restaurants.

Tamarind rice

The main ingredient in this hot and sour rice dish is tamarind, which comes from the pod of the tamarind tree. Other ingredients include lentils, chillies, curry leaves and spices such as cumin seeds, mustard seeds and black peppercorns. It is the tamarind that gives the dish its signature sour taste. Often garnished with roasted peanuts, this dish is best eaten hot with pappadam and raita.

Tomato rice

This simple yet delicious dish is prepared mainly with fresh tomatoes and a sprinkling of spices. It is garnished with finely chopped coriander leaves and served with accompaniments such as plain yoghurt, raita, onion salad or mint chutney.

Lemon rice

Among the more well known of south Indian rice dishes is lemon rice. This bright yellow dish is prepared with a variety of lentils (usually *urad* dal and Bengal gram dal), mustard seeds and peanuts; all these give the dish a crunchy bite. Its distinctive colour comes from the

liberal use of turmeric. Lemon juice is usually added to the rice when the dish is ready to be served. This dish can be eaten on its own or with raita and pappadam.

Coconut rice

This dish consists of steamed white rice with grated coconut, lentils, mustard seeds, red chillies and peanuts mixed into it. Coconut rice can be eaten with just pickles or pappadam. Or it can be eaten with *sambar* (see sambar rice).

PICKLES

South Indian pickles can be mild, tangy or fiery hot and are almost always soaked in *gingelly* oil (otherwise known as sesame seed oil) soured with tamarind, lime or yoghurt. The pickles are flavoured with mustard seeds, tamarind leaves and curry leaves. Where pickles continue to be made at home, they would be stored in airtight containers and can keep for well over a year.

Sambar rice

Sambar (right) is synonymous with south Indian food. It is a thick stew made with lentils (usually red gram dal) and vegetables such as radish, eggplant, carrots and drumstick. *Sambar* can be made with any combination of vegetables or with just one vegetable (each vegetable lends subtle differences in flavour). In either case, the vegetables are 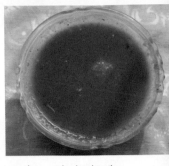 cut into small pieces and cooked together with the lentils. Some popular *sambar* dishes that can be found in Delhi are onion *sambar*, drumstick *sambar*, radish *sambar* and *sambar* with aubergines. To get *sambar* rice, simply pour *sambar* of choice over steaming hot rice… and enjoy!

Bisi bele bhath

Bisi bele bhath is a delicious and complete meal in itself and is usually served as a main course dish. Hailing from the southern state of Karnataka, this is a wholesome combination of rice, lentils, vegetables, cashew nuts and spices. *Bisi bele bhath* is a healthy meal because it is low in cholesterol and fat. Even then, it is not very popular among many north Indians.

Thali meals

Thali is the name given to a round or oval-shaped stainless steel rimmed plate. Food served on thali is ubiquitous wherever you go in south India. And one good way to enjoy southern cuisine in Delhi, especially if you like rice, is to order a south Indian thali.

A typical south Indian thali would contain a mound of white rice surrounded by at least six neatly arranged stainless steel bowls. Each bowl contains a small quantity of a different type of dish. Typically, these would be a *sambar* dish, rasam, a lentil dish, a vegetable dish, plain yoghurt or raita and the last, a sweet dessert. Most eateries will prepare a different variety of *sambar*, rasam and vegetables every day. In a basic thali meal, you will also get one piece of pappadam and some pickles. If the restaurant is generous you will get a small vada, too.

Thali meals offer value for money as you can have unlimited helpings of rice, *sambar*, rasam and vegetables without being charged extra. But such unlimited helpings do not extend to yoghurt, dessert or pappadam. Some south Indian eateries in Delhi even include puri into the meal. Some might also offer two types of thali. In such a case, the costlier one would fetch you probably two vegetable dishes, two pieces of roti, a banana and perhaps an extra dessert.

Whichever you choose, you can take out the small containers and put them on the table, which is what many locals do. This way, there is space for you to mix the rice with the accompaniments.

NORTH INDIAN THALI

North Indian thali meals are available in Delhi, but they are not popular perhaps because of the sheer variety of delicious north Indian cuisine. Such meals, though, are quite popular in the smaller northern towns. Where they are available in Delhi, they would be served on stainless steel plates and consist of north Indian bread such as roti, naan or paratha and several small bowls containing lentils, vegetables, a cottage cheese dish such as *palak paneer* or *shahi paneer*, yoghurt and a dessert. There will also be chopped onion and radish, pickles and a whole green chilli, which the locals gamely bite into. For some reason, papad is rarely offered.

Chutney

Chutney, like pickles, is an accompaniment that goes well with both north Indian breads and south Indian meals. They make food tastier. Because of the easy availability of coconuts in the south, coconut chutney (above) is the most popular of south Indian chutneys. Apart from coconut, its other ingredients are crushed red or green chillies, mustard seeds and cumin seeds. Delhi eateries serving south Indian fare usually offer coconut chutney and chilli chutney. In the north, mint chutney takes pride of place (this contains garlic, green chillies, tamarind paste, sugar and salt) followed by mango and tomato chutneys.

Light meals

Nothing epitomises south Indian food more than the humble dosa. When it made its appearance in Delhi, the only variety available was the plain dosa, which was seen as a simple breakfast and snack item and came with *sambar* and coconut chutney. Very quickly, along with the crispy vada, dosa became the top favourite for those seeking out south Indian cuisine.

In addition, restaurants began to merge the dosa with local tastes. As the size of dosa increased, so did the quantity of the masala that came with it, making dosa filling enough to serve as a complete lunch or dinner meal. Today, dosa comes in a myriad of shapes.

Apart from dosa (the popular ones are listed here), vada and idli are equally sought after in south Indian restaurants in Delhi. All of them come with the ubiquitous *sambar* and coconut chutney, which are provided gratis and in endless quantities. Many eateries will also offer mint and chilli chutneys.

Plain dosa

Dosa or *thosai* (as it is known in south India and countries like Sri Lanka and Malaysia) is, undoubtedly, a signature south Indian dish. Made from a batter of short grain *parmal* or *sela* rice and *urad* dal, and cooked on a *tawa* with a touch of oil or butter, dosa looks very much like a large crepe. It has to be eaten hot while it is still crispy. Because of their size (the average being about 25 centimetres long), dosa is almost always lightly folded into half (although some eateries present it in other creative ways). It is usually eaten with accompaniments such as *sambar* and coconut chutney. Some restaurants provide red chilli paste or chilli powder. In Delhi, the latter is affectionately called 'gun powder' because of the intense sensation it brings to the tongue.

Paper dosa

Paper dosa is dosa that comes as thin and crisp as a sheet of paper. It is the crispiest of all the varieties of dosa. When rolled, it can reach almost 45 centimetres in length!

Masala dosa

Masala dosa is dosa that comes with masala within its fold. 'Masala' is the term given to any type of mixture; in the case of dosa, this mixture usually consists of mashed potato and finely sliced onion, laced with chillies, mustard seeds and cumin seeds. Dosa with masala can be quite filling. You can even order a paper dosa with masala.

Mysore masala dosa

This special dosa hails from Mysore in the southern state of Karnataka. It is different from other dosa in two ways. First, butter and some Mysore chutney — a concoction of chillies, garlic and cumin — are spread on the dosa before the masala is added. The chutney gives the dosa a tangy and spicy taste. Second, the masala itself consists of extra ingredients such as tomatoes and beans. As usual, this dosa comes with coconut chutney and *sambar* on the side.

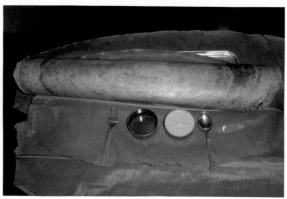

Rawa dosa

The difference between this dosa and the others is in the batter. *Rawa* dosa is made from a batter of lentils and *rawa*, or semolina (which gives the dosa a coarse texture) while the others are made with lentils and rice. *Rawa* dosa is often cooked with sliced onion, for which you get onion *rawa* dosa. You can also ask for onion *rawa* masala dosa, which comes with masala and onion. Like all other dosa, this dosa comes with coconut chutney and *sambar*.

Paneer masala dosa

Paneer masala dosa is a north Indian adaptation of the south Indian dosa. Instead of the usual potato and onion masala, a thin layer of paneer, or cottage cheese, is spread on the dosa to give it a rich taste. Again, *sambar* and coconut chutney will be given separately.

Idli

Idli is a white, spongy steamed cake (about 8 centimetres in diameter) made from a batter of mainy *sela* rice and *urad* dal. The batter, which is left to ferment for a few hours, is poured into special idli moulds and then steamed. Being light on the stomach, idli is popular among south Indians as a breakfast food although this is not the case with north Indians who prefer to have dosa or vada to start their day. As no oil is used, hospitals all over the country are increasingly making idli part of their menu. Idli is eaten with coconut chutney, 'gun powder' or *sambar*.

Vada

Vada is a deep-fried doughnut-shaped snack and is another popular south Indian treat. It is made from *urad* dal, which is first soaked in water and blended into a thick batter together with chillies, salt and some spices. The batter is shaped and then deep-fried until golden brown and crisp. Vada is especially tasty when eaten hot and dipped in coconut chutney and *sambar*.

Sambar vada

Sambar vada is vada that comes soaked in piping hot *sambar*. Coconut chutney is provided as an accompaniment. This is a treat that can be found at just about every nook and corner of the city, so much so that it has become a favorite snack with Delhites.

Dahi vada

Also known as curd vada, this is vada served in *dahi,* or plain yoghurt. It is most popular in summers because of the cooling effect that the yoghurt brings. Green chillies, cumin seeds and mustard seeds are often mixed into the yoghurt to give added flavour.

Uppuma

A very simple yet wholesome dish, uppuma is made by cooking semolina in a pan with chillies, diced vegetables (such as peas and carrots), curry leaves and, occasionally, peanuts and cashews. In India, it is popularly eaten at breakfast and any time in between. Although uppuma is tasty enough to be eaten on its own, it usually comes with *sambar* and coconut chutney.

Bonda

If you love potatoes, then *bonda* is for you! These deep-fried lime-sized potato balls are made from a mixture of *besan* (gram flour), crushed red and green chillies, ground mustard, ginger and coriander leaves. They make an excellent snack and are especially satisfying with a steaming cup of south Indian coffee.

Pongal

Although this dish is named after a popular south Indian festival that celebrates the harvest, it is one that is prepared every day. Not to be confused with *shakra pongal* — a dessert that also goes by the same name — this rice-and-lentil snack is normally served with *avial*, a thick gravy dish comprising mixed vegetables and grated coconut. Pongal, which looks very much like uppuma, is made with rice and dry roasted *moong* dal (green gram lentil), then pressure-cooked with cumin, ginger, black pepper and ghee. It is garnished with lightly-fried cashews.

Malabar adai

Perhaps the most famous of all south Indian snacks, *Malabar adai* is a pancake made from a mixture of rice and three different varieties of lentils. As the name suggests, this snack hails from the Malabar Coast in the southern state of Kerala. The lentils are soaked, ground to a paste and then shallow-fried with carrots, peas and onion. *Malabar adai* is served with *sambar*, coconut chutney and *avial*.

Uthampam

Uthampam is another popular breakfast dish from the country's south. It is so popular in Delhi that it is now eaten at all times of the day. It is a kind of pancake made from the same batter that is used for making dosa. However, it is smaller, thicker and more glutinous than dosa. A large spoonful of batter is poured on a *tawa* and spread evenly. When it begins to turn golden brown, it is turned over. Chopped onion, chopped tomatoes, minced chillies and ginger are then sprinkled on it. The most popular variety in Delhi is the tomato and onion uthampam. You can even get paneer uthampam, where the main topping is cottage cheese. Uthampam goes perfectly with coconut chutney and *sambar*.

Non-vegetarian

South Indian cuisine is not just about dosa or vada or other vegetarian dishes, even if these are preferred and more popular in Delhi. There are many well known delicious non-vegetarian dishes. Hyderabadi mutton biryani, for instance, is a truly well-regarded south Indian meat dish. Furthermore, the easy availability of fish and prawns in the south — particularly along the coast of Malabar in Kerala (a state known for spices) and Chettinad in Tamil Nadu — has led to the creation of equally mouth-watering seafood dishes. Yet, south Indian meat and seafood dishes are not popular in Delhi (where north Indian Mughlai chicken and mutton preparations reign supreme) and so, very few Delhi restaurants serve non-vegetarian dishes. Comparatively, south Indian meat dishes are spicier and hotter and their other main ingredients are coconut and oil.

Hyderabadi mutton biryani

As the name suggests, this popular dish comes from Hyderabad, a city in the state of Andhra Pradesh now better known for its IT industry. Apart from rice, the main ingredient is chunky pieces of boneless mutton marinated in yoghurt and ginger-garlic paste. When ready to be served, the rice is garnished with finely chopped onion, nuts and raisins (the last adds a tinge of sweetness to the dish). In some places, sliced hard-boiled eggs are added to the dish.

Kerala chicken curry

In this gravy dish, pieces of chicken breast are first coated with a paste of red chilli powder, turmeric, coriander powder, ginger and garlic. The meat is then fried in some oil with cloves, cinnamon, aniseed, curry leaves and sliced tomatoes. Water is added to form the gravy and the meat is left to cook. Coconut milk is added to give the dish a rich, milky taste.

In Andhra Pradesh, chicken curry is cooked not with coconut milk but with grated coconut, whole red chillies and whole spices such as cumin seeds, poppy seeds and fennel seeds.

Kerala fish fry

This easy to prepare dish is usually eaten with steamed rice. Here, mackerel is coated with red chilli powder, turmeric powder, black pepper, garlic, ginger and salt. The fish is then deep-fried in vegetable oil. Garnished with chopped raw onion and with a squeeze of lemon juice, this dish is very statisfying.

Kerala fish curry

With aromatic spices and coconut milk, this gravy dish is always a popular choice. Here, sliced pomfret is marinated in a paste of red chilli powder, curry powder, turmeric powder and fenugeek powder. The fish is then added to a pot where small onion, mustard seeds, fenugreek seeds and chopped garlic and ginger have been sautéed. Coconut milk is added just before serving. Some restaurants would add macaroni or sliced tomatoes to the dish.

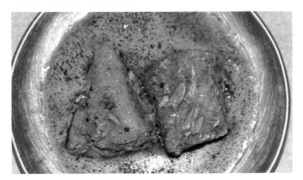

Desserts

As with north Indian desserts, south Indian desserts, especially its sweets, are legendary. They come in a riot of colours — creamy white, red, green, saffron, bright yellow and brown. Many sweets are wrapped in thin edible silver foil. Sugar, honey, milk and jaggery are the dominant ingredients of Indian sweets. The popularity of sweets in India has to do with religion; during major festivals hundreds of thousands of tonnes of sweets are produced and consumed. So much is in demand that shop owners have to display the sweets out on the pavement.

No south Indian dessert — or meal for that matter — is complete without a hot cup of south Indian coffee, served in stainless steel cups. The coffee powder comes from the Coorg region in the southern state of Karnataka. The coffee is brewed thick to which milk and sugar is added. If you want less sugar or want the coffee strong, let the waiter know.

Shakra pongal

This rice-based dessert is rich in taste and calories, thanks to the use of ghee and jaggery. Apart from being very sweet, the latter gives a distinctively greenish-brown colour. This thick and heavy dish is garnished with cashew nuts and raisins.

Payasam

A traditional south Indian meal is considered incomplete without a bowl of *payasam*, which is a pudding similar to the northern version known as kheer. This thick, creamy dessert is made with rice and milk, and flavoured with spices such as cardamom, nutmeg and saffron. Although *payasam* can be made with different ingredients, the most common is *plain payasam*, which

consists of just rice and milk. Other popular varieties are *semiya payasam* (made with vermicelli), *coconut payasam* and *rawa payasam* (made with semolina).

Kesri halwa

This sweet fudge (*halwa*) is easily recognised by its distinct orange colour that comes from saffron, or *kesri* as this expensive flavouring is known locally. The ingredients that go into making *kesri halwa* are *rawa*, or semolina, cardamom, saffron and butter. *Kesri halwa* garnished with cashews is a very traditional south Indian recipe.

Laddu

This is a well-known south Indian sweet but one that is not very popular in Delhi. Made of gram flour, saffron, cashews, raisins, sugar and rock candy, these lime-sized sweet balls are deep-fried and then placed in a sugar syrup. They are often served cold.

South Indian restaurants

Andhra Pradesh Bhawan Canteen

 1 Ashoka Road

2km; Andhra Bhawan building

🕒 7:30am–10:00am, Noon–3:00pm, 7:30pm–10:00pm

💲 Cash only

 📞 2338-7499

Popularly known as Andhra Bhawan, this restaurant is located in a nice tree-lined area not far from the India Gate memorial. Over the years, Andhra Bhawan has become synonymous with good south Indian food and has won a legion of admirers who seek out its reasonably priced vegetarian and non-vegetarian thali meals (the latter comes with chicken or mutton curry). Its weekend chicken biryani never fails to attract faithful customers.

Banana Leaf

📍 N12 Outer Circle, Connaught Place

Walking distance

🕒 10:00am–11:00pm

💲 💲 📞 Cash and credit card

 📞 5152-3777 / 2331-2355

Banana Leaf's prime location in Connaught Place means one thing: the restaurant is always crowded. But with such high turnover, the food is always fresh. Best selling items include curd rice, lemon rice, uppuma and *dahi vada*.

Coconut Grove

📍 Hotel Janpath, Connaught Place

Walking distance

🕒 11:00am–11:00pm

💲 💲 💲 Cash and credit card

 📞 2334-0070 / 2336-6105

Although dosa and vada are offered here, Coconut Grove is known more for its Kerala-style chicken and mutton curries. Another of its specialities is chicken Chettinad, a dish from Tamil Nadu state.

Dakshin

 Marriott WelcomeHotel, Saket

 15km

 12:30pm–3:00pm, 7:30pm–Midnight

      Cash and credit card

      2652-1122

Among the high-end hotel restaurants that offer south Indian cuisine, many Delhi residents consider Dakshin to be the best. Whether you need Kerala fish fry or the ubiquitous dosa or vada from Tamil Nadu and Karnataka, you will find excellent preparations at Dakshin.

Govardhan Restaurant

 93 Adchini, Aurobindo Marg

 12km; near Aurobindo Ashram

 9:00am–11:00pm

      Cash and credit card

       2651-3961 / 2653-3630

Located on a busy south Delhi road but one that is easy to find, Govardhan is a good place for south Indian cuisine. The favourites here are rasam, dosa, *dahi vada*, *andhra pesrattu*, uthampam and *Malabar adai*. After your meal, try a south Indian *meeta* paan.

Guru Prasad Udupi Restaurant

 DDA Shopping Centre, Munirka

 10km

 Noon–3:30pm, 7:00pm–11:00pm

        Cash and credit card

      2617-5487 / 2610-6572

Although this place sells popular north Indian food, its forte is south Indian vegetarian cuisine. Try its excellent idli and vada, but be prepared to dine in rather crammed conditions.

Hotel Saravana Bhavan

 46 Janpath, Connaught Place

 Walking distance

 8:00am–11:00pm

  Cash and credit card

  2331-7755 / 2331-6060

Already an established name in Chennai (Madras), Hotel Saravana Bhavan has taken Delhi by storm. It offers, among many other dishes, 20 varieties of dosa, rasam, a hearty thali and desserts such as pongal. You also get a different rice dish — coconut rice, lemon rice, tomato rice or tamarind rice — every day. One meal that it offers daily is the Quick Lunch, which consists of *sambar* rice, curd rice, rice of the day, vegetables, pickles, chips and sweet pongal. Unlike other south Indian vegetarian restaurants where you get extra helpings of *sambar* and chutney for free, here you will have to pay for them.

Kamakshi

 Hotel Samrat, Chanakyapuri

 5km

 7:00am–11:00pm

  Cash and credit card

  2611-0606

This restaurant offers good Kerala cuisine but for some reason, it is not that well known. Its most popular dishes are keema dosa, fish fry and *appam* with stew. Look out for the Prime Minister's official residence as you get nearer to the hotel.

Karnataka

 46/3 Yusuf Sarai Market, Aurobindo Marg

 9km; about 1km from the AIIMS hospital

 7:30am–11:00pm

  Cash only

 2686-2026

This small restaurant has been doing well for years, opening early every day and closing late. It is a favourite with both families and singles who do not cook at home. Its thali meals are good and so are the fluffy, filling vada and dosa. Karnataka also serves tasty north Indian puri and chole.

Karnataka Food Centre

Rao Tula Ram Marg, Sector 12, R K Puram

8km

7:30am–11:00pm

Cash only

2618-7357

This is a favourite haunt for Delhi residents who love south Indian food. The fastest selling items are *rawa* dosa, vada, curd rice and *bisi bele bhath*. Try the pongal, if it is available, as well as its other rice dishes which is never repeated on consecutive days. For coffee, you cannot go wrong with south Indian coffee but tell the waiter not to make it too milky.

Naivedyam

1 Hauz Khas Village, Hauz Khas

8km

11:00am–11:00pm

Cash and credit card

2696-0426

If you want a taste of south India (both in decor and cuisine), head for Naivedyam. Start your meal with rasam and pappadam and then try the dosa; some preparations come filled with cashew nuts. Its thali meals are good and *bisi bele bhath* is just what it should be. Dial-A-Meal service is available here.

Neelgiris

P 19/20 Pandav Nagar, Mayur Vihar Phase 1

10km

7:00am–11:00pm

Cash only

2275-6548 / 2279-2353

Although Neelgiris is located across the Yamuna River and far from the city centre, it is very popular. It is difficult to find fault with Neelgiris — its dosa, *sambar* vada, *dahi* vada and uthampam are very good.

New Keraleeyam

N 92/2 Pratap Market, Munirka

10km

11:00am–11:00pm

Cash only

2616-4362

If you cannot go to Kerala to enjoy its cuisine, the next best thing to do is to head for New Keraleeyam. Its fish curry is outstanding, and so is the *payasam*, which comes with the vegetarian thali. Other authentic Kerala dishes are available here and the restaurant boasts a loyal clientele.

Nirula's

L Block, Connaught Circus

Walking distance

10:30am–11:00pm

Cash and credit card

2341-7419

As the pioneer of Indian fast food in Delhii, Nirula's is still going strong, offering burgers and pizzas at affordable prices. If you are in Connaught Place and want a quick dosa or vada, go to Nirula's. The range of south Indian dishes may be limited, but they taste great. (See entry under north Indian restaurant listings on page 89.)

Sagar

18 Defence Colony Market, Defence Colony

7km

8:00am–11:00pm

Cash only

2433-3110 / 2433-3440

Until the arrival of Hotel Saravan Bhavan, Sagar faced little competition. Still people continue to dine at Sagar, which has a dozen branches in the city of which the one at Defence Colony is the most popular. All the items on its menu are good; even then the main demand is for rasam, thali, vada and dosa. However, be prepared to wrestle with the crowds. If you want to dine in a quieter environment, then consider its branch at Ashok Hotel in Chanakyapuri (tel: 2611-0101); there is hardly a crowd and the food is equally good, but you pay double the price.

SKR's Grand Sweets

 Rama Market, Munirka

 10km

 8:00am–10:00pm

 Cash only

      2616-4850 / 2618-2614

If you are not fussy about decor or ambience and if you want value-for-money meals, then this small restaurant is worth checking out. Not surprisingly, it is very popular with the south Indians who live in the area. Owned by a member of an extended family that has been in the catering business for decades, Grand Sweets is good for idli, vada, dosa and pongal. For dessert, try the *halwa* and laddu.

Standard Restaurant

 Regal Building, Connaught Place

 Walking distance

 11:00am–Midnight

      Cash and credit card

    2336-0048 / 2374-4688

Although known more for its north Indian cuisine, it also serves good vegetarian dosa and vada. Grab a window seat and watch the traffic below as you tuck into a satisfying meal.

Swagath Restaurant

 Defence Colony Flyover Market, Defence Colony

 7km

 11:00am–Midnight

     Cash and credit card

     2433-7538

This is the place where Delhites go when they want seafood and Indian coastal cuisine. Swagath's prawn biryani and chilli garlic butter crabs are its best selling dishes.

Udupi Café

Pratap Bhawan, Bahadur Shah Zafar Marg

4km

8:00am–11:00pm

Cash only

2335-3577

This no-frills eatery offers value for money provided you are willing to battle the crowds that throng there every day. The fastest selling items are dosa, vada, idli and uthampam.

'Chinese' cuisine

Like Mughlai food, Chinese cuisine has become a part and parcel of the Indian palate, particularly in the last two decades. It is second only to north Indian cuisine in terms of popularity. But the Chinese food known and enjoyed in India today is different — some would say very much so — from authentic Chinese fare, which is available in India but only at select hotels and restaurants. Even connoisseurs of the authentic variety have found the names of some Indian Chinese dishes (as well as their taste) strange, if not bizarre. Such is the difference between the Indian version and the authentic version that Chinese food in Delhi is often referred to as 'Indian Chinese food'.

One feature clearly brings out the difference between the Indian Chinese food and the authentic variety: Indian Chinese food is a blend of spices — often turmeric and garam masala — with Chinese sauces, especially soya sauce (of both the light and dark varieties) and red chilli sauce. These sauces are made locally (did you know that India cultivates its own soya beans?) with the Indian tongue in mind. Chilli sauce, for example, will be hotter.

Today, Chinese food is available in virtually every Indian city. It can be enjoyed in restaurants and wayside eateries; it can even be bought at small kiosks (below) and mobile vans, which the enterprising Indians have set up. In these places, do not expect to see too many Indians using chopsticks! As one Chinese restaurant owner, Amitabh Thakur, pointed out: "Very few customers ask for chopsticks. But once they try it and become adept at using it, they will ask for it the next time!" Forks and spoons remain the most commonly used cutlery in the city's Chinese restaurants.

ORIGINS OF CHINESE CUISINE IN INDIA

The roots of Chinese food in India can be traced to around 1780 with the early migration of the Chinese people. One of the first immigrants set up a sugar factory in Calcutta (Kolkata), then capital of British India, but the business failed shortly after. Although the man died heart broken, his Chinese workers stayed on and made India their home.

Nineteenth-century Calcutta was the nerve centre of a small but hardworking group of Chinese who took to shoe making, set up tanneries, ran laundry businesses, became dentists and, of course, started eateries to cater to the gastronomic needs of their own kind. When India became independent in 1947, the Chinese population stood at around 50,000. Most lived in Calcutta. However, their numbers fell with the 1962 Sino-Indian war, which saw the harassment and internment of many Chinese.

But it was also in the 1960s that Indians began to take an interest in Chinese cuisine. And once they fell for it, there was no holding them back! That interest quickly led to the growth of a new kind of cuisine, one that fused Indian flavours and traditional spices with Chinese style cooking, producing what in India has today come to be known as 'Indian Chinese food'.

With migration continuing particularly to Hong Kong, Canada, Australia, Taiwan and Sweden, the Chinese population today stands at just about 4000, many of whom hold Indian passports.

Soup

Soup is an integral part of the Chinese diet and no meal is complete without a bowl of steaming hot soup. The Chinese who settled in India brought with them this tradition, gradually introducing the idea of having soup into the Indian psyche.

As can be expected, the various types of soup that is served in Indian eateries have been adapted from the Chinese versions to suit local tastes. This is done through the judicious use of spices and condiments such as chillies, cloves and other spices. As is the case with north Indian cuisine, soup is taken as a starter in Chinese eateries. Two popular types of soup that share not only common ingredients but are served in both north Indian and Chinese eateries in Delhi are Creamy Tomato Soup and Chicken Soup (for explanations of these soups, see pages 39 and 41).

Tomato egg drop soup / chicken egg drop soup

This soup may look plain, but it has a hearty taste thanks to the vegetable stock simmered with sliced onion. Tomato puree, chopped tomatoes and some cornflour give it a rich and slightly coarse texture. When the soup is almost ready and while the heat is still on, an egg is broken and allowed to coagulate at the top. Just before the soup is served, it is flavoured with some vinegar and garnished with coriander leaves. For a non-vegetarian version, there is chicken egg drop soup.

Vegetable sweet corn soup

This simple yet popular soup consists of corn, spring onion, cloves, cardamom, cinnamon, pepper and some green chillies. All these are left to simmer in vegetable stock for about 20 minutes. Some restaurants may sprinkle soya sauce on the soup just before serving.

Vegetable mushroom soup

This is a watery but delicious concoction of button mushrooms and vegetables such as cabbage and diced spring onion. These are simply put together and boiled. The chef will add a pinch of salt, soya sauce and vinegar for taste.

Vegetable garlic soup

This soup is not as pungent or hot as it may sound. It is a mixture of vegetables (in this case shredded cabbage and chopped spring onion) and chopped garlic simmered together in vegetable stock.

Vegetable noodle soup

This soup comes in such large portions that it can easily be taken as a main meal. The usual vegetables are carrots, spinach and cauliflower. The noodles are mainly thin rice noodles, somewhat like vermicelli. Some eateries may add a little corn and butter. The soup is flavoured with white pepper, black pepper and salt. When ordering this soup, you can ask for more vegetables and less noodles.

Chicken hot and sour soup

This rich soup lives up to its name. It is both hot and sour, and these taste sensations are immediately registered. Shredded chicken breast, button mushrooms, cubes of paneer (cottage cheese), spring onion, carrots, green chillies, tomatoes and chicken stock make up this soup. Sometimes, an egg might be dropped into the soup and left to cook in the heat. The seasonings include white and black pepper, vinegar, soya sauce and red chilli sauce. Cornflour is added to thicken the soup a little.

Rice

It is difficult to say with certainty which dish is more popular in Delhi's Chinese restaurants — fried rice or noodles. Without doubt, though, Indians are heavy rice eaters. When it comes to rice, most eateries opt for the short grain and cheaper *sela* rice. Fried rice is prepared the traditional Chinese way: the rice is first steamed, allowed to cool and then stir-fried with other ingredients. Apart from fried rice, Chinese eateries offer plain steamed rice to be eaten with side dishes, both vegetarian and non-vegetarian. All rice dishes come with chopped green chillies in vinegar sauce, tomato sauce and chilli sauce (of both the green and red varieties). Porridge, which is ubiquitous wherever in the world Chinese food is offered, is not popular in Delhi.

Vegetable fried rice

In this dish, cooked rice is stir-fried over high heat with onion, beans and cabbage. Soya sauce as well as a dash of coriander powder is added during the cooking process to give flavour as well as colour. This dish is almost always eaten with side dishes such as chilli chicken and chicken Manchurian. If the eatery offers yoghurt, do not be surprised if you see a local diner mixing some plain yoghurt into his plate of fried rice!

Singaporean vegetable rice

As with vegetable fried rice, rice is stir-fried with a mix of diced vegetables such as carrots, cabbage and spring onion, and seasoned with soy sauce and a dash of black pepper. This time, an egg is broken into the rice and cooked with it. Garnishing the dish are crispy deep-fried garlic chips, a condiment that makes it most tasty… and different from the others.

Egg fried rice

The ingredients that go into this dish are the same as those used for vegetable fried rice. The only difference is the addition of egg. This time, though, the egg is not cooked with the rice (as in Singapore vegetable rice). Instead, the egg is beaten separately and fried into an omelette, then cut into strips and placed on top of the dish. Unlike vegetable fried rice, which is usually eaten with side dishes, this rice dish is more often eaten as a main dish on its own. It is served with green chilli sauce and cut green chillies in vinegar.

Mexican vegetable rice

What is a Mexican rice dish doing in a Chinese eatery, you may wonder? Well, this is just one example of the bizarre names given to Chinese dishes in Delhi. In this dish, the rice is first cooked but not completely so that it does not become mushy when it is further cooked with the vegetables. It is then transferred to a wok where it is quickly stir-fried in a paste of chilli oil (extracted from

red chillies), garlic, chilli powder, garam masala and vegetable stock. The vegetables usually used in this dish are pineapple, cucumber, tomatoes and spring onion.

Chicken fried rice

This rice dish is prepared in a different manner from the others. Here the ingredients — boiled chicken fillets and chopped spring onion — are not stir-fried together with the rice. Instead they are tossed in rice that is already cooked. Other vegetables may be added. Finely chopped ginger, green chillies, white pepper, soya sauce and salt are thrown in for taste.

Noodles

Noodles have taken India by storm. So popular are they that supermarket shelves in Delhi and other big Indian cities bulge with packets of instant noodles, each containing its own seasoning. Small Indian restaurants and roadside eateries use locally made *maida* (plain flour) noodles. In pricey restaurants, imported rice and egg noodles are used.

In Delhi's Chinese eateries, you can get two main types of noodle dishes. The first is chowmein, in which noodles are stir-fried with vegetables and/or meat and eggs. Many locals would order a side dish of vegetables or meat to go with a plate of chowmein. But whether or not side dishes are ordered, most eateries will offer tomato ketchup and chilli sauce as accompaniments.

The second noodle dish is chopsuey. This is basically a dish of stir-fried vegetables on a bed of deep-fried crispy noodles. The noodles are first boiled with a pinch of salt and then deep-fried in vegetable oil until they turn light brown in colour. Chopsuey is so filling it is often eaten as a meal on its own.

Vegetable chowmein

This stir-fried dish is so popular in Delhi that many people see it as *the* dish that defines Chinese food in India. It is also one of the easiest and quickest to prepare. Finely shredded vegetables — usually onion, cabbage, carrots and capsicum — and noodles are cooked in vegetable oil in a wok. Salt, pepper and soya sauce are

added to flavour the dish. Delhi cooks will omit the soya sauce for customers who want their noodles 'white'.

Vegetable chilli garlic chowmein

This stir-fried vegetarian dish is perhaps as popular as the vegetable chowmein. The method of preparation is similar; the only difference lies in the ingredients and the oil used. Here chilli oil (extracted from red chillies) replaces vegetable oil, and plenty of finely chopped garlic and green

chillies are added. The inclusion of garlic and chillies makes this a rather hot dish, which may not suit those who cannot handle chillies well.

Singaporean chowmein

Singaporean chowmein, or Singapore rice noodles, is another popular noodle dish. This is one chowmein dish where rice noodles are invariably used. The ingredients include red chillies, black pepper, finely chopped garlic and spring onions. Soya sauce is not used. The dish is garnished with cut red chillies and fresh coriander leaves.

Egg chowmein

An egg lovers delight, this is actually vegetable chowmein with eggs. The eggs are separately scrambled or fried into an omelette (and cut into fine stripes), and then added to the egg noodles as the dish is being cooked. Some restaurants would add extra ingredients such as onion and capsicum.

Chicken chowmein

Here, the dominant ingredient is shredded chicken. This stir-fried noodle dish also contains shredded spring onion and finely sliced capsicum (of the green, red and yellow variety). When ready, the dish is garnished with some coriander leaves.

Vegetable chopsuey

Here, fresh vegetables such as carrots, capsicum, onion and cabbage (and sometimes Chinese lettuce) are fried in a wok with garlic. Seasonings like tomato paste, vegetable stock, white pepper, salt, sugar and some vinegar are added to the vegetables. When the entire mixture thickens, it is poured over noodles that have been quickly deep-fried. Vegetable chopsuey has a slight sweet and sour taste.

Egg chopsuey

This is essentially vegetable chopsuey with eggs added as a garnish. Often, two eggs would be used to make an omelette; this is then cut into strips and placed on top of the dish.

Chicken chopsuey

This dish consists of chicken and vegetables. Chicken breast is cut into small cubes, marinated in soya sauce and minced garlic, and then fried. As the meat begins to brown, vegetables such as cabbage, carrots, capsicum and onion are added. Care is taken not to overcook the vegetables. When ready, the vegetables are poured over the noodles.

American chopsuey

This dish is different from the others in that the vegetables — usually carrots, broccoli, cabbage, button mushrooms and baby corn — are steamed and not stir-fried. They are seasoned with ginger, garlic, tomato puree, soya sauce, chilli sauce, white pepper, salt and sugar. In some places, peanut butter might be added. The vegetables are then placed on top of deep-fried noodles.

Side dishes

In addition to noodle and rice dishes, Chinese eateries in Delhi prepare a variety of vegetarian and non-vegetarian side dishes. Although these are meant to accompany plain steamed rice, many Delhites prefer to have them with a plate of fried rice or chowmein. Most side dishes are stir-fried and come in thick gravy, with cornflour being the thickening agent. And unlike traditional Chinese cooking where sesame oil is often used, this flavouring is not commonly used in India. Here is a sample of some of the more popular Chinese dishes offered in Delhi.

Sweet and sour vegetables

This is an all-time winner. The main vegetables are bell peppers, button mushrooms, bamboo shoots and baby corn. These are stir-fried with some garlic, following which tomato ketchup, tomato puree, pineapple, sugar and vinegar are added. The latter two give the dish its sweet and sour characteristics respectively. The ingredients are then left to simmer until the gravy thickens. This dish goes very well with any of the fried rice preparations.

Vegetable chilli gravy

This dish can be fiery hot if the chef is allowed to have his way but is perfect for those who like their food this way. Vegetables such as beans, capsicum and cauliflower are cut into small pieces and sautéed in vegetable oil with lots of finely chopped green chillies. Some cornflour is added to thicken the gravy. When ready to serve, the dish is garnished with spring onion. For

those who want the dish less hot, the chef will use whole chillies instead. This way, the chillies can be easily taken out.

Vegetable ginger

Finely chopped onions and ginger form the mainstay of this dish. These are stir fried with carrots and left to simmer in vegetable stock. The seasonings include chilli sauce, soya sauce and a sprinkling of vinegar. When ready, the dish is often garnished with plenty of shredded ginger.

Paneer chilli

Paneer chilli is an excellent example of how the best of two culinary cultures have come together. Cottage cheese is first cut into cubes and deep-fried, then sautéed in oil with sliced onion, capsicum and green chillies. The ingredients are left to cook in gravy seasoned with soya sauce, vinegar and black pepper. This dish makes a perfect complement to fried rice.

Paneer Manchurian

Here again, cottage cheese is used. Small cubes of paneer are deep fried until their edges turn slightly brown; this hardens the outer layer of the cottage cheese while retaining its inner softness. The paneer is then quickly stir-fried with ginger, garlic, spring onion, tomatoes and green chillies. Chilli sauce and soya sauce are finally added. Fresh coriander leaves are used for garnishing.

Chilli chicken

Whichever Chinese eatery you go to in Delhi, chilli chicken will surely be on the menu; it is the most recognised of all Indian Chinese dishes. It is a stir-fried dish of small tender pieces of chicken, green chillies, onion and tomatoes in a gravy of corn flour and soya sauce. Before the chicken is stir-fried with the other condiments, it is first quickly doused in hot oil to seal in the juices. This very spicy dish goes well with plain steamed rice or vegetable fried rice.

Ginger chicken

In this dish, chicken drumsticks are first marinated in yoghurt and then stir-fried with garlic, green chillies, chopped onion and plenty of ginger. The drumsticks are turned in the wok until they turn slightly brown. Again, coriander leaves are used for garnishing.

Garlic chicken

Here chicken is first stir-fried with plenty of chopped garlic and left to simmer in a gravy flavoured with vinegar, soya sauce and salt. Unlike ginger chicken, the dominant flavour here would be garlic. Both ginger chicken and garlic chicken dishes make excellent companions for rice and noodle dishes.

Sweet and sour chicken

This dish consists of chicken breast pieces, carrots, capsicum and onion in a thick sauce. It is undoubtedly one of the more popular dishes in Delhi. Thanks to a wide variety of ingredients such as grated ginger, lemon juice, vinegar, garlic powder, pineapple slices, milk and sugar, it commands the perfect sweet and sour taste. Served hot, it goes very well with rice.

Lemon chicken

In this dish, fillets of chicken breast are first marinated in lemon juice, then dipped in cornflour and finally quickly immersed in hot oil. This deep-frying process not only seals in the natural juices of the flour-coated chicken, it gives a crisp coating to the meat while keeping the flesh tender. The chicken pieces are then stir-fried with finely chopped ginger and garlic, and slices of red, yellow and green capsicum. Some chicken stock is added. This colourful dish has a tangy taste and goes very well with vegetable fried rice and Singaporean vegetable rice.

Chicken Manchurian

In this dish, shredded chicken is marinated with ginger and garlic paste, vinegar, soya sauce, salt and white pepper powder and then stir-fried in vegetable oil until they become tender. Then honey, chicken stock, chopped celery, soya sauce and cornflour are added. The ingredients are left to simmer till the sauce thickens. This gravy dish is served hot, and goes very well with both plain rice and fried rice.

Shredded lamb in hot garlic sauce

In this dish, mutton is shredded and marinated in soya sauce, vinegar, egg yolk, pepper, salt and cornflour. The meat is then stir-fried in chilli oil (with white pepper and salt) until they become tender. Shredded vegetables like capsicum, onion and finely chopped garlic are added. When the dish is ready to be served, hot garlic sauce is poured over it.

Chilli lamb

People who like their food chilli hot often choose this dish. Here, tender pieces of mutton are stir-fried with ginger, garlic, onion, cut green chillies, cumin seeds and coriander leaves. This is left to simmer in some water. Chopped tomatoes and red chilli sauce are added to complete the taste.

Snacks

Indian Chinese restaurants also provide two fine snacks — *momos* (steamed Tibetan dumplings) and deep-fried spring rolls. There is no doubt though that *momos* are way ahead in terms of popularity especially among the young. A plate of *momos* usually comes with eight dumplings, each the size of a lemon. You will usually get four crispy pieces of spring rolls in a plate. You can get both types of snacks in vegetarian and non-vegetarian versions. These snacks are always eaten with green chilli sauce and finely chopped green chillies in vinegar. Momos are also very popular in neighbouring Nepal and Bhutan.

Vegetable momos

Momos may have originated in Tibet, but they have found a firm place in the Indian Chinese menu. The dough in the Tibetan version is made of roasted barley but in India, the dough is made from *maida* and water. It is rolled into small flat discs, each about 5 centimetres in diameter. Each disc is filled with finely shredded boiled vegetables such as cabbage, carrot, ginger and spring onion seasoned with pepper and salt. It is then folded over and crimped to seal before they are steamed for about 15 to 20 minutes. *Momos* are always steamed but restaurants also offer a fried version, in which case steamed *momos* are deep-fried in vegetable oil. If you see red chilli sauce on the side, beware as it is almost always blazing hot!

Chicken momos

Here, minced chicken replaces the vegetables. The filling would also consist of finely chopped onion and garlic, black pepper, salt to taste and a pinch of vinegar. These are also served with green and red chilli sauces. You can get pork *momos* in some places.

Vegetable spring rolls

These taste most delicious when dipped in chilli sauce. The dough for the spring roll sheet is made from *maida* and cornflour. A ladleful of dough is poured on a hot *tawa*, where it cooks somewhat like a pancake. When the sheet is ready, it is neatly filled with a row of finely shredded vegetables such as cabbage, arrots, capsicum and spring onion (some eateries add

mushrooms to the filling). The sides are folded in, after which the bottom corner is rolled over the filling. It is then placed into hot vegetable oil and deep-fried till golden brown and crispy. Each roll is chopped into four or five pieces and served with chilli sauce.

Chicken spring rolls/egg spring rolls

In chicken spring rolls, shredded chicken breast is added to the same vegetable stuffing that is used to make vegetable spring rolls. Egg spring rolls are also available, but

these are not as popular as the vegetable or chicken varieties. Again, these spring rolls come with green chilli sauce and finely chopped green chillies in vinegar.

Chinese restaurants

Aka Saka

📠 28 Defence Colony Market, Defence Colony

🧭 7km

🕐 Noon–11:30pm

💲 💲 💲   🧾 Cash and credit card

abc 🏠   ☎ 2433-3821 / 2433-3163

A popular restaurant in the district, Aka Saka serves spicy Chinese fare. People who dine here rave about the soups it serves. One soup that does good business is Aka Saka clear soup which comes with mushrooms, chicken, eggs, prawns and even pork. Other popular soups are *talu mein* (noodle soup with shredded meat and vegetables), tomato egg drop soup and clear chicken soup. Its chilli chicken and chicken garlic dishes may have a distinct Indian taste, yet they are always in much demand. Dial-A-Meal service is available here.

Belle Momo

📠 9 Scindia House, Connaught Circus

🧭 Walking distance

🕐 11:00am–11:00pm

💲 💲   🧾 Cash only

abc 🏠   ☎ 2331-7288

This small restaurant specialises in *momos*, preparing them with chicken, mushrooms and vegetables. Its affordable prices means it is a hit with office workers. A 'combo meal' consisting of soup, fries, ice cream and your choice of *momos* costs just Rs.120.

Berco's

📠 E8 Connaught Place

🧭 Walking distance

🕐 Noon–11:00pm

💲 💲   🧾 Cash and credit card

abc 🏠   ☎ 2341-8134

Affordable prices and a central location are the main reasons for the popularity of this restaurant. It serves very tasty American chopsuey and vegetable chopsuey, as well as vegetarian and non-vegetarian spring rolls. Dial-A-Meal service is available here.

China Garden

M73, M Block Market, Greater Kailash II

12km

12:30pm–3:30pm, 7:30pm–Midnight

Cash and credit card

2922-3456

Popular dishes here are its sapo chicken (chicken with garlic served in a clay pot over a burner), pepper prawns, tiger prawns with hot garlic sauce and pepper garlic prawns.

Chopsticks

Asian Games Village Restaurant Complex, Siri Fort Marg

10km

12:30pm–3:00pm, 7:30pm–11:00pm

Cash and credit card

2649-2348 / 2649-3945

This restaurant enjoys the support of loyal customers who vouch that it has maintained its standards since it opened. Popular dishes on its menu include chicken Hakka noodles, fish with ginger, prawns in garlic sauce and chicken in chilli garlic.

Chungwa

M Block Market, Greater Kailash II

12km

Noon–Midnight

Cash and credit card

2921-3477 / 2921-7877

Chungwa is a spacious restaurant and one of the more popular restaurants in south Delhi. Some of the dishes that are perpetually in demand are chicken in oyster sauce, chicken salt and pepper, crispy lamb with sesame seeds and Mandarin fish. Among the popular vegetarian dishes are vegetable Manchurian and spicy beancurd with aubergine. This place also whips up Thai food. Dial-A-Meal service is available here.

Daitchi

 E19A South Extension II

 10km

 Noon–11:00pm

      Cash and credit card

     2625-7511 / 2625-5381

Opinions differ about this restaurant but there are many who think it serves good Chinese food. Its spicy Shanghai chicken is said to be tasty. One of its popular dishes is chicken tomato stewed rice.

Drums of Heaven

 S14 Green Park

 8km; opposite Uphaar Cinema

 12:30pm–3:30pm, 7:00pm–11:30pm

      Cash and credit card

     2685-5963

Located next to the Deer Park, this restaurant is a popular venue for those who like Chinese food. Some well-liked dishes on its menu are chicken Mongolian and chicken fried rice.

Fa Yian

 A 25/5 Middle Circle, Connaught Place

 Walking distance

 Noon–3:30pm, 7:00pm–11:30pm

       Cash and credit card

     2332-3237 / 2332-3272

A family-run establishment, Fa Yian has been a favourite for many Delhi residents ever since it opened in Connaught Place. The Fa Yian Special Rice comes with spicy vegetables or chicken. Two excellent soups it offers are *talu mein* and Fa Yian Special (a tangy blend of creamed corn, mushrooms, vegetables and glass noodles). Dial-A-Meal service is available here.

Fujiya

 12/48 Malcha Marg

 7km; near Chanakyapuri

 11:30am–11:00pm

                                 Cash and credit card

                2687-6059 / 2611-3143

This restaurant, located in Delhi's diplomatic enclave, is always busy. And the reason for it has to do with the good food it offers. On its menu are a variety of poultry, pork and seafood dishes. The appetisers include wonton soup, shark's fin soup, chicken mushroom soup and noodle soup. Also on the menu are a variety of chowmein and chopsuey dishes. True to its name, Fujiya also serves Japanese cuisine. Dial-A-Meal service is available here.

Ginza

 K11 Outer Circle, Connaught Place

 Walking distance

 11:00am–11:30pm

                              Cash and credit card

                  5151-3129

Although this restaurant has a Japanese name, it serves mainly Chinese food. Customers go to Ginza for its soups, in particular the shark's fin soup, *talu mein* soup and hot and sour soup.

Golden Dragon

 C Block Main Market, Vasant Vihar

 12km

 Noon–11:30pm

                      Cash and credit card

                                 2614-1849

Another favourite haunt with Delhites, the most popular dishes here are chilli chicken and shredded lamb in hot garlic sauce. Dial-A-Meal service is available here.

House of Ming

📇 Taj Mahal Hotel, Man Singh Road

✇ 4km

🕓 12:30pm–3:30pm, 7:00pm–Midnight

💲 💲 💲 💲 💲   🖩 Cash and credit card

abc   ☎ 2302-6162

Its location in the exclusive Taj Mahal Hotel means two things: the food is expensive but you can be assured of getting authentic Chinese cuisine.

Huckmann's

📇 J Block Market, Saket

✇ 14km

🕓 11:00am–10:00pm

💲 💲   🖩 Cash only

abc 🏠   ☎ 2656-6984

An unpretentious eatery, Huckmann's is very popular with the locals because of its economical prices and good food, especially its soups. The chefs are obliging enough to whip up dishes to suit your taste. Do visit if you are watching a movie at the nearby PVR Saket. Popular dishes on the menu are steamed _momos_, egg chowmein and paneer Manchurian.

Imperial Garden

📇 E3 Local Shopping Centre, Greater Kailash II

✇ 12km

🕓 Noon–Midnight. Dinner only on Mondays and Tuesdays

💲 💲 💲 💲 💲   🖩 Cash and credit card

abc 🏠   ☎ 2922-7798 / 2922-7288

According to several food critics, this is the place to go for the finest and authentic Cantonese cuisine. Loyal diners say that its crab and lobster dishes are unparalled. The highlights of its menu are chicken roast, chicken Mongolian and sugarcane prawns.

Jade Garden

The Claridges Hotel, Aurangazeb Road

4km

12:30pm–2:30pm, 7:30pm–11:30pm

$ $ $ $ $ Cash and credit card

abc   2301-0211

A favourite with business executives, this Chinese restaurant is located in a nice garden in one of Delhi's prettiest hotels. Popular items on its menu are Sichuan prawn fried rice, lobster with five spice powder, ginger chilli chicken and crispy sliced lamb.

Larry's China

Ambassador Hotel, Sujan Singh Park, Lodi Road

6km

12:30pm–2:45pm, 7:30pm–11:30pm

$ $ $ $ Cash and credit card

abc   2463-2600

Run by the same Taj Hotel management which operates the House of Ming, this is another place of choice for Delhites who love Chinese cuisine. Although the verdict is divided over the authenticity of the food it serves, most customers agree that its soups are excellent.

Memories of China

48 Community Centre, New Friends Colony

15km

Noon–3:00pm, 7:30pm–11:30pm

$ $ $ Cash and credit card

abc   5167-2346

With efficent service and Master Chef Sitangsu Chakravarty's eye on the menu, this restaurant does good business. Among its popular dishes are chilli chicken, chicken in bean sauce, chicken Manchurian, almond vegetable and *chasa* chicken in red wine.

Nanking

 C6 Vasant Kunj

 17km; opposite Delhi Public School

Noon–3:00pm, 7:00pm–11:00pm

       Cash and credit card

     2613-8936

Nanking is highly recommended for its meat-based dishes especially steamed fish, steamed chicken in lotus leaf, sliced fish Mandarin and chilli crab. The restaurant promises to waive the cost of any dish should it not be to your liking. Although located some way out, Nanking is worth visiting. It also has a reputation for providing excellent service.

Nirula's

 L Block, Connaught Circus

 Walking distance

10:30am–11:00pm

     Cash and credit card

      2341-7419

The pioneers of Indian fast food in Delhi, Nirula's also has a commendable Chinese section where you get to sample a cross-section of Indian Chinese food.

Pioneer's Flavours of China

 H40 Outer Circle, Connaught Place

 Walking distance

11:00am–11:00pm

     Cash and credit card

   2373-8891

There must be something right about this place as it is perpetually crowded. It serves the usual Chinese fare, which is said to be prepared by Tibetan chefs trained by Chinese chefs. Not only are portions large, the cooks are willing to customise dishes to suit different tastes.

Princess Garden

🖭 E32 South Extension II

✤ 10km

🕐 Noon–11:00pm

💲 💲 💲   📠 Cash and credit card

🔤 🏠   ☎ 2433-3493

Located in a busy and crowded market, Princess Garden attracts shoppers. Its most popular dishes are lobster in hot green sauce, Hakka noodles, chicken Manchurian and crispy fried duck. Dial-A-Meal service is available.

Suribachi

🖭 Panchshila Rendezvous, Malviya Nagar Road

✤ 12km

🕐 Noon–Midnight

💲 💲 💲 💲 💲 💲   📠 Cash and credit card

🔤 🏠   ☎ 2668-2222

Another popular eatery for people in the neighbourhood, Suribachi scores with its crab in chilli oyster sauce, shredded potato in spicy sauce and beancurd in black bean sauce.

Taste of China 👨‍🍳

🖭 N18 Connaught Place

✤ Walking distance

🕐 Noon–11:00pm

💲 💲 💲   📠 Cash and credit card

🔤 🏠   ☎ 2371-4022

This restaurant comes highly recommended and is said to offer authentic Chinese fare. Popular dishes are steamed *momos*, stir-fried vegetables, Singapore chicken, crispy lamb and chilli chicken.

Tibetan Dhabas

 Majnu ka Tila

 15km; near ISBT Bus Terminus

 11:00am–11:00pm

   Cash only

    None

This is not one restaurant but a string of eateries with a fun ambience and casual atmosphere. It is very popular with students of Delhi University. Try the *momos*, soups and chowmein, of which there is a wide variety.

Trip to Beijing

 A13 Vishal Enclave, Rajouri Garden

 15km

 Noon–3:30pm, 7:00pm–11:00pm

     Cash and credit card

    2546-2200

While opinions differ as to the authenticity of the food, few doubt its quality. Try the chicken in hot garlic sauce, chicken Beijing-style and *kung po* rice chicken. Although located away from the tourist circuit, it is popular in the neighbourhood for its Chinese dishes. The restaurant also serves Thai food.

Zen

 B25 Connaught Place

 Walking distance

 11:00am–Midnight

     Cash and credit card

2335-7444 / 2335-7455

Zen is one of the few older and more spacious establishments in Connaught Place. On the menu are mainly Chinese dishes although it also offers a limited range of Japanese food. Food critics recommend its *sukiyaki* chicken and Sichuan prawns. Dial-A-Meal service is available here.

NON-INDIAN CUISINE

Asian

Baan Thai (Thai)

 The Oberoi Hotel, Zakir Hussain Marg

 7km

 Noon–3:00pm, 7:00pm–11:30pm

💲 💲 💲 💲 💲 💲   📠 Cash and credit card

   ☎ 2436-3030

Rather expensive restaurant but one that many Delhites consider is the place to go for Thai cuisine. The most popular dishes are *thod man koong* (prawn cakes with plum sauce) and *poo cha* (deep-fried crab meat with minced chicken).

Bangkok Degree 3 (Thai)

 C49 50 Shopping Complex, Defence Colony

 7km

 11:30am–3:30pm, 7:30pm–11:30pm

💲 💲 💲   📠 Cash and credit card

     ☎ 5155-0233

Culinaire (Thai/Lebanese)

 Chandan Market, Greater Kailash II

 12km

 Noon–11:00pm

💲 💲 💲   📠 Cash and credit card

    ☎ 2921-2414

Patrons dine under a tin shed in this quaint open-air eatery, which is popular with families for its authentic Thai and Lebanese cuisine.

Ego Thai (Thai)

🍴 53 Community Centre, New Friends Colony

✛ 15km

🕐 12:30pm–3:30pm, 7:30pm–Midnight

💲 💲 💲 💲 💲   💻 Cash and credit card

𝑎𝑏𝑐 🔺   ☎ 2633-1181

This is another favourite place for Thai cuisine and one that gets a good crowd despite hefty prices. It serves vegetarian fare without onion or garlic, as well as the usual meat-based dishes.

Enoki (Japanese)

🍴 The Grand, Nelson Mandela Road, Vasant Kunj

✛ 16km

🕐 Noon–3:00pm, 6:30pm–Midnight

💲 💲 💲 💲 💲   💻 Cash and credit card

𝑎𝑏𝑐   ☎ 2677-1234

Kumgang (Korean)

🍴 Hotel Ashok, Chanakyapuri

✛ 8km

🕐 11:00am–3:00pm, 7:00pm–11:00pm

💲 💲 💲 💲 💲 💲   💻 Cash and credit card

𝑎𝑏𝑐   ☎ 2611-0101

Oriental Octopus (several cuisines)

🍴 India Habitat Centre, Lodi Road

✛ 5km

🕐 12:30pm–3:00pm, 8:00pm–11:30pm

💲 💲 💲   💻 Cash and credit card

𝑎𝑏𝑐   ☎ 2468-2222

This restaurant is popular for the simple fact that one can try the cuisine from five countries: Indonesia, Korea, Malaysia, Thailand and Vietnam.

Suribachi (Japanese)

 Panchshila Rendezvous, Malviya Nagar Road

 11km

 Noon–Midnight

       Cash and credit card

      2668-2222

Tamura (Japanese)

 D8 Poorvi Marg, Vasant Vihar

 12km

 Noon–11:00pm

       Cash and credit card

      2615-4082

Thai Wok (Thai)

 109/1 Rooftop, Ambawatta Complex, Mehrauli

 16km

 Noon–3:30pm, 7:00pm–Midnight

       Cash and credit card

     2664-4289

Turquoise Cottage (Thai/Chinese)

 81/3 Adchini, Aurobindo Marg

 12km

 Noon–Midnight

        Cash and credit card

      5250-0200

Dial-A-Meal service is available here.

Zen (Japanese/Chinese)

 B25 Connaught Place

 Walking distance

 11:00am–Midnight

  Cash and credit card

 2335-7444 / 2335-7455

Non-Asian

All American Diner (American)

 India Habitat Centre, Lodi Road

 5km

 7:00am–Midnight

  Cash and credit card

  2468-2222

Basil & Thyme (European)

 Santushti Shopping Complex, Chanakyapuri

 7km; opposite Hotel Samrat

 10:30am–6:00pm. Closed on Sundays

  Cash and credit card

  2467-3322

Culinaire (Lebanese/Thai)

 Chandan Market, Greater Kailash II

 12km

 Noon–11:00pm

   Cash and credit card

 2921-2414

Patrons dine under a tin shed in this quaint open-air eatery, which is popular with families for its authentic Lebanese as well as Thai cuisine.

Flavors (Italian)

 DDA Shopping Complex, Defence Colony

 7km; under Moolchand Flyover

 11:00am–11:00pm

 Cash and credit card

 2464-5644

La Piazza (Italian)

 Hyatt Regency, Ring Road

 12km

 Noon–3:30pm, 7:00pm–11:00pm

 Cash and credit card

   2679-1234

Lodi, The Garden Restaurant (Continental/Middle Eastern)

 Lodi Road

 6km; next to Lodi Gardens Gate 1

 12:30pm–11:00pm

 Cash and credit card

 2465-5054

This glass-encased restaurant is superbly located in the beautiful Lodi Gardens, probably Delhi's best kept garden. The desserts are especially good.

Moshe's Oliva (Mediterranean)

 The Capital Court, Munirka

 10km

 10:00am–11:00pm

 Cash and credit card

5166-8696 / 5166-8697

Regular diners at this restaurant rave about its Spinach Crepe and Wild Rice.

Nirula's (Italian)

 L Block, Connaught Circus

 Walking distance

 10:30am–11:00pm

      Cash and credit card

     2341-7419

For an Italian pizza with a difference, try Nirula's where the pizzas have a distinct Indian taste.

Rodeo (Mexican)

 A12 Connaught Place

 Walking distance

 Noon–Midnight

     Cash and credit card

  2371-3780

San Gimignano (Italian)

 Hotel Imperial, Janpath

 Walking distance

 12:30pm–3:00pm, 7:30pm–11:30pm

       Cash and credit card

     2334-1234

Shalom (Lebanese/Mediterranean)

 N Block Market, Greater Kailash I

 10km

 12:30pm–3:30pm, 7:30pm–Midnight

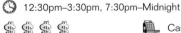   Cash and credit card

 5163-2280 / 5163-2281

TGI Fridays' (Mexican/American)

 Basant Lok Complex, Vasant Vihar

 12km

 Noon–11:00pm

           Cash and credit card

          2614-0761

TGI Friday's has a branch in the heart of Delhi. Head for F16 Connaught Place (tel: 2371-1991)

The Big Chill (Italian)

 F38 East of Kailash

 12km

 Noon–11:00pm

           Cash and credit card

          2648-1030

Posters of 1950s Hollywood films adorn the walls to give this restaurant a great atmosphere. Its pastas, as well as the chocolate mousse, are a hot favourite among the youths of Delhi. There is another branch nearer the city centre at 68A Khan Market (tel: 5175-7599).

Celebrity chefs

A chef with a mission

Meet Master Chef Sitangsu Chakravarty, a man who wanted to study science but ended up becoming one of north India's most renowned chefs. Born into a middle class family and intent on studying science, Chakravarty never dreamed of making his career whipping up mouth-watering Indian dishes. On the advice of a family friend, he took up a course in hotel management in New Delhi and joined the India Tourism Development Corp (ITDC) where he opted to learn cooking. Within a year he fell in love with Indian cuisine and headed for New York's Culinary Institute of America to widen his knowledge and hone his skills.

Despite the fact that Indian cuisine has taken the world by storm, the effervescent 56-year-old asserts that it is still burdened by several misconceptions. "Outside India people do like Indian food, the taste, the aroma, and realise the medicinal value of the spices," Chakravarty says, sipping a steaming cup of Darjeeling tea at his New Delhi home filled with curios collected from around the world. But there are problem areas, he admits, and offers his own reasons.

One reason, he offers, is that Indian cuisine remains a poor cousin to French, Mexican, Italian and even Chinese cuisine because it is just not being marketed as it should be. The second reason is that the term 'spicy', which is always used when describing Indian food, is widely but wrongly seen as synonymous with being 'chilli hot'. The third reason, which he sees is the biggest drawback and which puts off many people, is the heavy use of oil and fat.

"There is a certain logic against Indian cuisine," he admits. "It is too greasy, too oily, too heavy. And the oil settles in the stomach, making Indian food heavy."

It is this that Chakravarty has vowed to correct. And he has pursued this goal with a vengeance for the past 30 years, whether in New Delhi, Mumbai, Bangalore, Kolkata, Jaipur, New York, London, Sri Lanka, Yemen or Oman. Wherever he went, he constantly strived to make Indian food lighter and more palatable for those who consider it too heavy. And, he says with a tinge of pride, he has succeeded to a great extent. He must have because he does have quiet a fan club today.

"For me the challenge was how to reduce fat in Indian food," he says. "You cannot do away with fat because there is natural fat in everything: coconut, yoghurt, fish, chicken. The point is to avoid additional fat so that the food is lighter and the flavour is more intense, in a natural way." Chakravarty calls his no-added-fat-food the 'Pure Flavour' cuisine.

Contrary to popular belief that Indian food cannot exist without oil or ghee, Chakravarty argues that the opposite is true — that the flavour becomes intense when oil is kept away or kept to the barest minimum. "I don't fry, I roast," he explains. Oils and fat, he says, soak up more than 30 per cent of the taste, in addition to affecting aroma and colour. Through careful selection of herbs and spices, precision timing in the cooking process and dry roasting the foods in their own juices rather than frying them in oil, he vows to change the diner's attitude towards Indian food.

Do people like the food he cooks?

"Of course, yes!" is Chakravarty's response. "I make contemporary Indian food very modern, very presentable, very glamorous! I am also exploring Indian regional cooking. India is, after all, a continent by itself and probably no other country has such a wide culinary vocabulary. In fact cooking oil was hardly an item in original Indian cuisine. That is an invention of commercialisation. The dishes I make are lighter, which attracts people to come back and try them again."

Today, Chakravarty keeps himself busy providing consultancy services — including menu development and planning — to three restaurants: Café Masala (predominantly north Indian cuisine), Memories of China (authentic Chinese cuisine) and Rodeo (Mexican fare). In addition, he writes cookery books and hosts cookery programmes on television. "My aim," he says with a touch of finality, "is to develop Indian food into a world cuisine."

(Sitangsu Chakravarty resides in Delhi and can be reached at this e-mail address: sitangsu_chakravarty@yahoo.co.uk)

Café Masala

 A12 Connaught Place

 Walking distance

 Noon–Midnight

      Cash and credit card

      5528-5749

This is Delhi's first weigh-and-pay restaurant. You get to choose what you want and the quantity from a selection of dishes spread out buffet-style. Except for roti, which is charged by the piece, rice and side dishes are sold by weight. Vegetarian dishes cost Rs.18 per 100 grams, while meat dishes cost Rs.30 per 100 grams. With the menu overseen by Master Chef Sitangsu Chakravarty, you can be sure of getting your money's worth.

Memories of China

 48 Community Centre, New Friends Colony

 15km

 Noon–3:00pm, 7:30pm–11:30pm

      Cash and credit card

       5167-2346

With efficent service and Master Chef Sitangsu Chakravarty's eye on the menu, this restaurant does good business. Among its popular dishes are chilli chicken, chicken in bean sauce, chicken Manchurian, almond vegetable and *chasa* chicken in red wine.

Rodeo

 A12 Connaught Place

 Walking distance

 Noon–Midnight

        Cash and credit card

        2371-3780

Rodeo specialises in Mexican cuisine.

If it's tandoori, it must be Karim!

On the streets of Delhi's crowded old quarters, Aleemuddin Ahmed might be mistaken for an ordinary middle class Muslim resident, perhaps a small-time trader. But make no mistake — Aleemuddin is a grand old man who weaves magic with Mughlai cuisine.

In 1958, when Aleemuddin was 23 years old, his father (the late Nooruddin Ahmed) decreed it was high time his son entered the kitchen of the family restaurant to master the art of Mughlai food. Aleemuddin, now a grandfather, did just that... and more, making Karim a landmark restaurant and one synonymous with delectable Mughlai cuisine.

Today, Karim — located in a congested lane near the historic Jama Masjid — is probably the first choice of connoisseurs of spicy mutton and chicken delights. Over the years, it has spawned many copycats in the area but none stands up to it in quality, aroma and taste.

Yet when Karim opened in 1913, it was not even known in the neighbourhood. It was a small eatery offering only three items: dal (lentil curry), *aloo gosht* (potato and lamb) and roti (flat north Indian bread). It was a modest beginning, but those were times when eating out was not considered respectable and only visitors to the city who did not have a host bought their meals from eateries and restaurants. But the quality of its fare ensured that it did not fold up. By the 1950s, Karim's popularity spread mainly by word of mouth. As a consequence, it opened new outlets and expanded the range of dishes on their menu. Today, it has two dine-in outlets as well as three takeway outlets.

"There is no doubt that we gave renewed oxygen to Mughlai cuisine," says the bearded Aleemuddin Ahmed, describing himself as an owner-chef. Seated next to him is his son, Wasiuddin Ahmed, now a vital part of the Karim empire. "In the 1950s we came to be known for our mutton korma, mutton stew and chicken curry. People were drawn to us. The city was rediscovering Mughlai food, and saw it as a vital part of Indian cuisine. In the process, the people discovered Karim."

Aleemuddin is in love with chicken and mutton, and has a positive dislike for anything vegetarian although his restaurant serves many vegetarian dishes, too. "Vegetarian food," he says, "is for the chicken hearted!" With such conviction, it is no wonder that Karim has today become firmly identified with — and remains so despite growing competition — succulent chicken, mouth-watering tikkas and peppery spice-laced lamb that melt in your mouth. There is *yakhni* soup, which is extracted from meat and bones and which Karim loyalists say is out of the world. There is rumali roti and sweet kheer, a dessert served in earthen cups. Another favourite of the regulars is *tandoori bakhra*, which is lamb stuffed with chicken, rice, eggs and dried fruit.

"Our recipes are top secret," asserts Aleemuddin, comparing himself to a magician who will exhibit his talent to the public but not reveal the secrets. "Some of our dishes require as many as 33 spices! We don't mind revealing what the spices are, but for now our secrets will remain with us!"

Aleemuddin never tires of telling the story of a man who, after a hearty dinner at Karim, insisted on kissing the hands of the master chef. "Let me kiss the hands that make such delicious food!" the visitor insisted. Aleemuddin explains: "The magic is in the right proportion of everything we put in, not just the ingredients. It is skill that we learnt from our forefathers. If we are good, it is all because of Allah!"

(Aleemuddin Ahmed can be reached at this e-mail address: khpl@del3.vsnl.net.in)

Karim

🍴 Gali Kababiyan

🧭 10km; near Jama Masjid

🕐 Noon–3:30pm, 6:30pm–11:30pm. Closed on Tuesdays

💲 💲 💲   📠 Cash and credit card

   ☎ 2326-9880 / 2326-4981

This is Karim's main outlet and it serves delicious Mughlai food, a must for anyone who loves chicken and mutton. Every dish on the menu is worth trying but I would recommend the chicken curry, *murgh mussalam* and chicken tikka. Take a stroll after your meal around the congested but lively area around the restaurant. Nearby is Jama Masjid and not far away is the imposing Red Fort. Note that Karim and its three other outlets do not serve lunch during the Muslim fasting month of Ramadan. Dial-A-Meal Service is available. Karim has another dine-in outlet at Hazrat Nizamuddin (West) and three takeaway outlets.

Dastarkhwan-e-Karim (second dine-in outlet)

🍴 168/2 Jha House, Hazrat Nizamuddin (West)

🧭 7km

🕐 Noon–3:30pm, 6:30pm–11:30pm. Closed on Mondays

💲 💲 💲   📠 Cash only

Takeaway outlets

🍴 1 & 2/5 Sagar Complex, Vikas Marg, Preet Vihar

☎ 2221-9517 / 2220-6311

🍴 18/85 Zakir Nagar, near New Friends Colony

☎ 2698-1619 / 2698-0565

🍴 A 18 Kailash Colony

☎ 2646-7868

Index by restaurant name

Index by local food item

About
the Author

M. R. Narayan Swamy has been a journalist for the last 27 years and is currently the Chief News Editor of the Indo-Asian News Service (IANS) in New Delhi. In 1994, he published *Tigers of Lanka*, a chronicle of Tamil militancy in Sri Lanka and the Liberation Tigers of Tamil Eelam (LTTE). He then followed the book's success by writing *Inside an Elusive Mind*, the first biography of LTTE Chief Velupillai Prabhakaran. This was published in 2003.

It was Narayan Swamy's love of Indian food and his innate curiosity that led him to undertake the challenge of writing a food guide. To him, it was the perfect opportunity to explore more of his hometown of New Delhi and spend time indulging in one of his favourite pastimes.